THE NEW NATURALISTS

Inside the Homes of Creative Collectors

THE NEW NATURALISTS

Inside the Homes of Creative Collectors

with over 300 illustrations

Claire Bingham

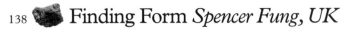

INTRODUCTION

The New Naturalists at Home

There are some naturalists who love archives. They love the history and orderliness and the process of classification, and find pleasure in taking a single item from the shelf to study for the day. Every single facet, they are amazed.

There are others who gather memories. They are nostalgic – for childhood, family histories, a certain place or time, a feeling that transports them back to early thought processes and helps them gain an understanding of who they are. You can't really remember yourself as a child; other people remember you. But it's through these objects and early fascinations that you recollect what was important to you at that time.

Some collectors fall into the category of those who just pick things up. They might find beauty in river stones worn smooth by the water or jagged shards of limestone, rich in quartz, or feel gratification in a rock's solidity or in its curved, palm-fitting form. From this, there is a design to create patterns, with an artistic appreciation of colour, shape and texture, and for how structures actually work. No one does this better than Mother Nature. A bucketful of scallop shells with their gradation of pink and burgundy shades are wonderful in their uniformity and individuality – no two are the same. It is this enjoyment of the 'perfect/imperfect' that drives these enthusiasts' artistic endeavours.

Each room in Sean Barton's 19th-century gatehouse in Cheshire is filled with ferns and orchids, a particular passion. *Previous pages* On the wall of Peter Adler's London home is a pair of ceremonial hats from the Bamileke people in Cameroon, made from dyed chicken feathers.

At the dealer end of the spectrum, collectomania comes from the need to discover something and possess it, a compulsion facilitated from a lifetime of learning and a highly tuned eye. Collectors take a fragment of the past and reimagine its future, in effect becoming a caretaker of its time. Hoarders, curators, dealers, foragers, tinkers and dreamers – the urge behind the fetish of collecting and the meaning within someone's individual swag is a psychologist's dream. It's like entering into their inner world.

Inspired by the naturalists and cabinets of curiosities of the 19th century, as well as the shell-encrusted grottoes at places like Woburn Abbey in Bedfordshire, or the souvenir-filled home (now museum) of Sir John Soane in London, a new generation of collectors are decorating their homes with their finds, everything from fossils to crystals to shells. In these pages, we are given a glimpse into their homes to discover the world's most interesting natural collections and how these objects can be used to transform interiors. With our ever-increasing interest in sustainability and search for new ways to reconnect with nature, *The New Naturalists* will be inspirational reading for all those who want to celebrate nature in their homes and the pleasure of stuff.

Anyone can begin a collection. It doesn't have to be at the museum-worthy end of the scale. Here, we look at homes from all over the world – different collections, different aesthetics – with each story bound to one person's obsession for collecting and magpie urge to acquire. From a compact house in Berlin (Maggie Coker; pp. 198–207), crowded with dried flowers in every corner, to a bejewelled London interior where talismans, fossils and minerals are carefully balanced (Carol Woolton; pp. 96–105), these homes prove that too much is never enough. The more creative and eccentric, the better.

The artist Michele Oka Doner (pp. 158–67) gives a tour of her striking New York apartment, where every curve and crevice is layered with history and discovered finds. In the Parisian home of sculptor Zoé Rumeau (pp. 36–43), collected feathers and bones have been used to create mythical beasts. And the beautifully styled abode of architect and artist Spencer Fung (pp. 138–47) is decorated with simple, soulful objects that have been gathered over the years, many of them foraged from the beaches of his childhood home in Hong Kong. Driftwood, pebbles and salt crystals have found their place in the natural, tactile decor, creating harmony and balance, inside and out. Spencer's home is an especially inspiring example of how thoughtful, slow living can be used to imbue an environment with the warmth, elegance and sensuality that are becoming his signature.

With nature as the lead designer, the way that each person displays their collections varies wildly. For some, the most important step is to organize like with like, while others prefer the deliberate juxtaposition of ancient forms and contemporary art. Still others like consistency, using motifs from nature as recurring features, in much the same way that some might use colour to tie a scheme together. Those at the bohemian end of the scale love accumulation, but not necessarily order. It's not a stretch to imagine that a person who loves natural history is going to have something extraordinary going on. These magician's lairs, where snowy owls cast their gaze over

AFTER ALL, THERE ARE A HUNDRED MILLION YEARS OF INSPIRED DESIGN TO SHOP FROM. WHAT CAN BE MORE HOLISTIC THAN THAT?

elegant tableaux and lizard-like plants seem to sprawl out from glass bell jars, reflect the characters of those highly creative people who collect out-of-the-ordinary specimens and pay tribute to them in their homes with an art director's eye.

Collecting is about being aware of who we are through the things we are drawn to – and being responsible, while not overly worried about what anyone thinks. This heart-on-sleeve type of accumulation is not concerned with fashion or the instant gratification of buying something from the shops. It is deeper-seated than that, especially important in our busy digital age. The point with all of these things is that you have to be patient – there's no fast-tracking. It's hard to find the right thing, for the right space, at the right size. After all, there are a hundred million years of inspired design to shop from. What can be more holistic than that?

Oliver Gustav's tiny, light-filled home in Copenhagen is the ideal setting in which to show off his collections of objects and works of art. *Overleaf* In Michele Oka Doner's New York apartment, an enormous plan chest dominates the open space and provides plenty of surface area for display.

MENAGERIE

THE HOME OF THE ANCESTORS
Emma Hawkins, Edinburgh, UK

Have you ever wondered what it must be like to live in a museum? In this home belonging to one of the world's most pioneering antiques dealers, the rare and exotic inhabit the entire space, like a pantheon of treasures from the natural world. Moving freely between artefacts with a historic presence and important works of contemporary art, the outstanding items on display range from the extinct to the just-born. The effect is curated, not cluttered, achieved by an intense focus and a very good eye. The interior is all about showcasing the weird and the wonderful, coupled with a strong aesthetic sense that makes the whole house spectacular, too.

This exceptionally stylish room is bursting with treasures from the world of natural history, displayed as forms of sculpture. Emma thinks of herself as a keeper of the natural world from a time when we weren't so in tune with rare and endangered species and the planet we inhabit.

Filled with weird and wonderful creatures, the living room features a snowy owl perched on top of a sculptor's stand and a tangle of antlers, spilling out over the floor. The large, stainless-steel lights were salvaged from Spitalfields Market in London when it closed down.

There aren't many people who have one of the earliest Tudor marbles in existence – a marble statue of a dog – in their hallway. The objects in this home can take you anywhere in the world, back to any time, even to places of extinction. Both home and retail space, this three-storey archival interior opposite the Royal Botanic Garden in Edinburgh is home to antiques dealer Emma Hawkins, whose lifelong interest in natural history inspired her to open a museum in northern Scotland. When it closed, she filled up her home and garage instead, turning the bespoke storage in her dining room into a cabinet of curiosities.

'I like that juxtaposition of eating while surrounded by objects of intrigue,' she says. 'The collection lends itself to candlelight. If there's ever a lull in the conversation at dinner, you can admire what's in the cabinets. It makes for an interesting evening.'

Emma collects rare artefacts of outstanding beauty, from taxidermy to jewelry, furniture and clocks. Her obsession for possessing examples of natural history began early, as her father is the esteemed rare art and antiques dealer John Hawkins, who was head of the Australian Antique & Art Dealers Association and known throughout the world for his zoomorphic finds. 'The seed was very much planted when I was a baby,' she explains. 'I lived and breathed among all of these influences and objects.'

From the age of twelve, Emma followed her father throughout the antiques world in Britain, cutting her first deal (a pair of Polynesian paddles) with a dealer in Norwich. 'Since then I haven't really looked back,' she says. 'There's a sadness that the world of antiques dealing as it once was – from the 1980s when I entered it – is no more. Those big country houses, where they used to have four-day sales just for the contents of the attic, don't exist anymore. Most of them are National Trust properties now or the money's

been spent, from generation to generation. That world has become extinct, but I try to keep a piece of it alive in my home.'

The trigger for Emma is the fantasy of the past and bringing it into her house. 'I was asked once by a museum to explain why I thought this was such a good piece, and I said that I just get the vibe,' she says. 'They replied that it's very difficult to footnote a "vibe"! It comes from the tactile nature of something or its shape. It's something I want to own, so I'll buy it. With the more modern things, I look for items with longevity that give me the nod it's not going anywhere.'

One of her most treasured items is a whole egg of the extinct elephant bird, a flightless species from Madagascar that stood at 4 m (12 ft) in height. 'It shows life and fragility,' Emma says. 'David Attenborough's documentary very much got me into those, and I'm lucky to own a full, unbroken egg.'

Collecting is an act of creation, and Emma has created this environment in her own home, layering the space and installing those objects she finds most beautiful. Many of the pieces are mighty, but the house has a lovely softness to it, from the grey colour palette to the use of textiles, foxed mirrors and display of natural forms. 'My personality and drive are on the masculine side, yet I hope I come across with some feminine wiles,' she says. 'It's important to have that mixture.'

An architect helped to design the wide spaces with symmetry, providing the perfect base for Emma to incorporate old and new. Here, no scrimping is in evidence. 'That's my Achilles heel,' she admits. 'Everything has to be perfect. I even put crystals under the floor to make sure the house has the right energy. It's important and nice to know what you're walking on.'

Emma's home is calm yet full of intrigue, but most of all a space you want to return to – much like a really good museum.

'I LIKE THAT JUXTAPOSITION OF EATING WHILE SURROUNDED BY OBJECTS OF INTRIGUE.'

In the combination kitchen/diner, the museum-feel comes from the cabinets, which Emma commissioned from a local cabinetmaker following her design. The floor is Italian marble and wenge wood.

EMMA'S
GUIDE TO
BUYING
TAXIDERMY
WITH CARE

1 Always consider what you are buying and for what reason. I lean towards objects that tell a story or are unusual, but are also texturally interesting and with good colour.

2 Research the dealer or retailer to ensure you are buying from a good source. Taxidermy is a skill. There are good taxidermists and poor ones, exactly the same as with artists. You have to be aware of what you're buying.

3 Make sure you have the right legalities. Any reputable taxidermist will ensure that no birds or animals have been killed to order. Each animal will have died naturally and sourced from zoos, safari parks or breeders, with strict documentation to prove it.

4 Remember that taxidermy is a decorative art, which allows the animals to retain their essence of life. There is nothing gruesome or cruel about it. Rather than just being dust in the ground, taxidermy restores a creature to its finery. Hopefully, its soul is resting in the right place.

'THE COLLECTION LENDS ITSELF TO CANDLELIGHT.
IF THERE'S EVER A LULL IN THE CONVERSATION AT DINNER,
YOU CAN ADMIRE WHAT'S IN THE CABINETS.'

EMMA HAWKINS

LIVING INSIDE A CABINET OF CURIOSITIES
Hubert Zandberg, London, UK

There are people who live inside their heads and find white walls and minimal interiors inspiring. Then there are others, more extrovert, who prefer to be surrounded by colour and things. This home falls into the later category. Conceived as a full-size cabinet of curiosities, the interplay between natural artefacts, modernist design and contemporary art is highly individual and mostly about style. Reflecting the owner's African roots alongside European art, this interior isn't concerned with creating an inventory of the natural-history world. Instead, the collection is about how objects communicate with each other, bringing continents, cultures and epochs together as one.

Display cases – found or custom-made, contemporary or reclaimed from shops – have been used to form cabinets of curiosities all over the house. The grouped objects coalesce into a single piece, to bring balance to a room or keep the clutter under control, allowing the eye to take everything in.

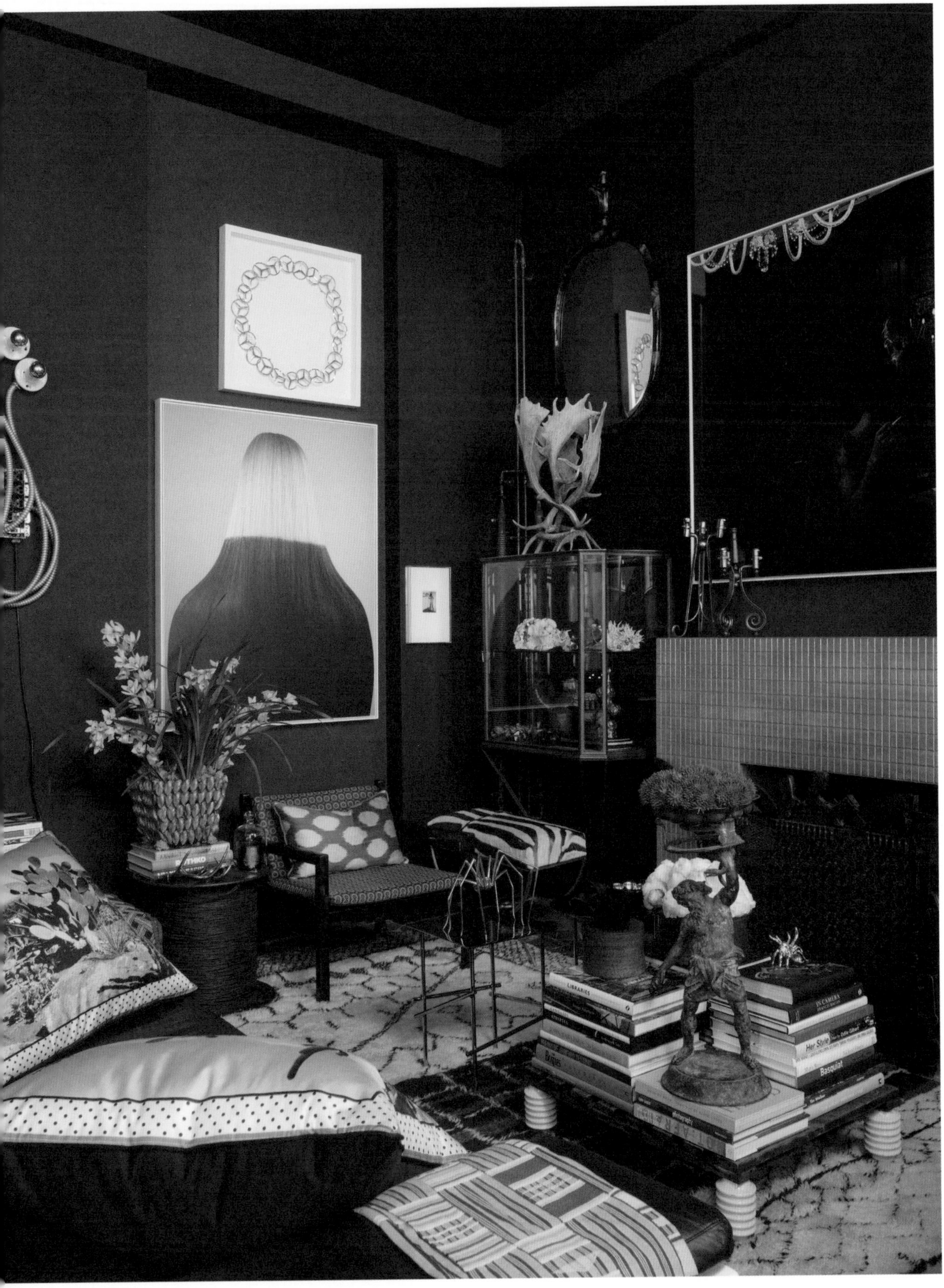
LIBRARIES
Her Style
Basquiat

The striking backdrop of African objects, colourful artworks and idiosyncratic pieces are arranged in considered vignettes. On either side of the fireplace, the layout is symmetrical, with a bookcase designed by Bruno Peinado dividing the space and providing more surface area for display.

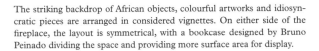

'I don't collect things to categorize or to focus on one aspect,' explains interior designer Hubert Zandberg, whose love of collecting natural history has its origins in a childhood spent in South Africa, layered with a taste for Brazilian modernism and European art. 'For me, it's to do with the relationship of objects and their dialogue together. I could go to a museum to look at every example of a cowrie shell if I wished. In my own home, that's not what I'm after at all.'

What drives this individualist designer and collector is the desire to use pieces as building blocks for creating a narrative, and he will happily segue from the primitive to the modern, northern hemisphere to southern, bringing the ripple effects of his life and interests together like a beautiful storm. It's dense, it's eclectic, and there are many moods. 'I become a conductor, making a symphony of all of these notes,' he says. 'That's what makes collecting interesting for me.'

When it comes to manipulating space with collected items, there has to be relevance. If Hubert was to come across the most beautiful shell on the beach, he would only pick it up if he knew where, or how, he was going to use it. 'If not, there's no reason for me to have it,' he explains. 'It's the same with buying pieces. There are many spectacular items that I would love to own, but if I don't see a context within the hegemony of what I'm creating, then it's not for me. It's for someone else.'

Growing up on a farm in the Karoo desert, immersed in nature, formed Hubert's early experience of aesthetics, scale and culture. 'If you had an interest in art, it was all to do with bird's nests, stones and porcupine quills,' he says. 'My first cabinet of curiosities really happened when I was about five or six, gathering rocks. When I look back on those things now, it's a feeling of pure nostalgia.'

Informed by time spent among the indigenous Khoisan people as a child, Hubert's views on taxidermy are that it is a celebration of nature. 'When it became all the rage in the art world and every artist jumped on the bandwagon to have a dead animal in their installation, some did it with more respect and success than others,' he says. 'Soon after, all the restaurants were full of it. For me, that was for all the wrong reasons. It was a fad and diminished my relationship with the pieces that I have. Times change. What was perhaps OK a while ago may be not so OK now. The jury is still out on that one, but it's something I always think about when appropriating natural history and bringing it into my home.'

And for those who want to channel a similar vibe, combining a trove of eclectic works of art with a flair for the flamboyant, Hubert's advice is to keep the scheme monochromatic. His living room, painted inky blue to showcase the white natural pieces, plays the juxtaposition card wonderfully, with the contrast emphasizing their beauty. Each room has a different story, giving insight into a beautiful, imagined world.

'They say your personality is formed by the age of four,' Hubert says of his passion for acquiring treasures from the natural world. 'I look at my collections and can absolutely see that my personality was formed back then. Once a collector, always a collector.'

'I COULD GO TO A MUSEUM TO LOOK AT EVERY EXAMPLE OF A COWRIE SHELL IF I WISHED. IN MY OWN HOME, THAT'S NOT WHAT I'M AFTER AT ALL.'

'Collections are best displayed en masse,' Hubert says. All-white items, including a whale vertebra, coral pipes and a hippopotamus skull, are grouped together against the dark blue walls of the living room. Beneath the stairs is a collection of miniature ladders from the Dogon tribe in Mali.

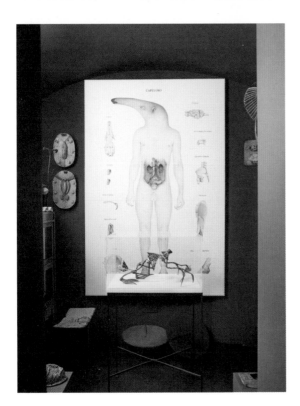

In the bedroom, a chest and coffee table act as cabinets of curiosities, while the headboard features a traditional Zulu skirt, along with a crucifix and an abstract work. The interior of the house has a mostly neutral colour palette, allowing the natural textures of Hubert's collections to stand out.

Hubert's decorative taste is 'more is more'. Vintage red mirrors from the Porte de Clignancourt flea market in Paris are hung beside a custom-designed four-poster bed. Fabric from the Venetian firm Rubelli forms the canopy, and the butterfly throw is from Kokon To Zai.

HUBERT'S
TIPS FOR
BUILDING A
COLLECTION

1 Don't worry about the monetary value of objects. Beauty and inspiration can be found all around us, and nature offers the most inexpensive treasures if we allow ourselves to 'see'. Treat your prized shell as you would a Fabergé egg.

2 Be true to yourself and collect things that you love. By doing so, you ensure the longevity of your collection. Nature is never out of style.

3 For a successful and captivating collection, think about what represents your life and love. Try holding on to items that hold a narrative of your life and memories.

4 To create interesting dialogues, try juxtaposing disparate objects, cultures, epochs and styles. This gives new meaning to the pieces, and the collection becomes more than the sum of its parts.

5 Try combining items from nature with contemporary art. If you use colour as an unexpected backdrop, this is an easy place to start.

6 Let the collection dictate the decoration of a room. Look at the shapes, colours and textures, and then add furniture to the space around it.

7 Be brave. A collection with a clear direction, narrative and point of view is always dynamic and inspiring.

8 To contain smaller collections, it is a good idea to use a display case. You can create a cabinet of curiosities in the most minimal of spaces.

HUBERT ZANDBERG

'MY FIRST CABINET OF CURIOSITIES HAPPENED WHEN I WAS ABOUT FIVE OR SIX, GATHERING ROCKS.'

A MENAGERIE OF FANTASY AND FEATHERS
Zoé Rumeau, Paris, France

Artist and designer Zoé Rumeau is a sorceress when it comes to creating fantastical sculptures from collected finds. She gathers all types of raw, natural materials, and uses them along with linen and leather to create her folkloric animal heads, which are displayed on the walls of her apartment in Montreuil, in the eastern suburbs of Paris. A rag-and-bone lady at heart, she hunts for antiques on holidays, and when travelling to India, always brings back a souvenir.

Framed beetles, old wooden shoes and hand-dipped wax candles adorn the peacock-patterned walls. Feathers, horns and leather offcuts are hand-stitched to create beast-like mannequins, and twigs are woven and coerced into the light sculptures for which Zoé is most known.

The dreamy bathroom features a mirror from Zoé's grandparents' house and beautiful twigs and branches, set against a dark-painted wall. All of the plants were chosen deliberately to give the feel of a jungle, as the apartment doesn't have any outdoor space.

'I HAVE SO MUCH FUN CREATING ANIMALS
BECAUSE THERE IS SO MUCH PERSONALITY YOU
CAN GIVE THEM.'

For Zoé Rumeau, collecting is all about the thrill of the chase, and never knowing what she will find next. She is at her happiest visiting Jaipur in India, where she sources all sorts of knickknacks to bring home and put to good use. 'I get most of my materials from India,' she says. 'My sister settled there twenty years ago, so I visit several times a year. Every time I go, I bring back things.'

Zoé is predatory when it comes to flea markets and foraging for fallen things – her treasures might include a box of brass sequins, which she entwined with willow branches to fashion the enormous pendant light that dominates the living space. Razor-clam shells and split bamboo feature in her studio, as do feathers from every type of bird. She has a huge index of artisans and dealers all over the world from whom she sources the most curious items, but it is in India that she does most of her rummaging. The dried marigold garlands, taxidermy peacock and a whole lot of silver leaf all came from there and remind her of her family.

Known for transforming an array of organic materials into sculptures that intertwine animal, botanical and manmade forms, it's this fusion that gives character to her artworks. The surreal eeriness of Zoé's patchwork wild horse in the bathroom, for example, is striking in both size and form, and she combs through feathers, hair and branches to summon up her phantasmagorical installations for clients such as Bonpoint and Baby Dior. 'I have fun creating animals, because there is so much personality you can give them, from a sense of humour to sadness,' Zoé says. 'It is so satisfying.' It's no wonder that the sculptor Louise Bourgeois is an influence.

'When I have a piece of wood, I look at it and think about how I can take it further,' Zoé explains. 'I've always mixed wood with gold leaf, with woven hair. I don't like fake things. I'm vegetarian, yet I work with bones. I love the energy of these raw, esoteric materials, but I can't explain why.' Although she grew up in the city, she says that she has always had strong ties to nature. 'My mother's family lived by the sea in Spain, so we were always there during the holidays, looking for pebbles and picking up all sorts of flotsam and jetsam that had been swept onto the beach. I'd live by the sea if I could.'

Sitting in her loft apartment, surrounded by framed series of beetles, porcelain dolls, feathered beasts and souvenirs from India, Zoé is a true Parisian eccentric. The inside of her home is both modern and reflective of her personality, telling the story of where she's been and where she's going.

'Initially, it was a just a white cube,' she says. 'My husband designed it to keep the sense of volume, so that the space works well. On the main floor, the kitchen, living room and dining room are all open to let the energy flow. At the top level are the children's rooms with windows overlooking the living room, and curtains for privacy should they need them. My husband is a carpenter, and he made most of the furniture. For my part, my sculptures are scattered throughout the house.'

The decoration of the apartment came first, and Zoé incorporated her collection, rather than having it dictate the decor. The books, framed pictures and plants, as well as the Hanuman masks and other *objets trouvés*, speak of Zoé's love of the magical, as well as her magpie eye.

A pendant light made from tangled branches and brass sequins makes the most of the high ceilings. In contrast to the patterned wallpaper, furnishings have been kept minimal. Chairs designed by Giancarlo Piretti sit alongside a drawing by Zoé herself, a work in progress for an exhibition at Galerie Laure Roynette in Paris.

Zoé's interest in natural history and folk-inspired curiosities is evident throughout her apartment and studio. Fallen nests from a nearby forest, along with foraged nuts, branches and feathers, all serve as inspiration for her work.

ZOE'S
HINTS FOR
DISPLAYING
COLLECTIONS
WITH AN
ARTIST'S EYE

1 Don't get hung up on any one piece's meaning or use. I love the shape of the candles hanging from my wall because they remind me of the bones of my sculpture. It's nothing to do with the fact that they are candles.

2 Don't be too precious. Have fun mixing different types of objects, of all sorts of value.

3 To create an atmosphere, try to position collections in unusual places. I do this with my animal sculptures as if they were real and just passing through.

4 For a dynamic effect, display items en masse. To show items off in the bathroom or kitchen, collections look better against a dark background, rather than a clinical white one. I also like to hide away toiletries, so that they don't detract from the items on display.

5 Cast a stunning glow on objects by covering a wall in silver leaf. I did this in the bedroom, and it was a beautiful solution for this dark space. A humble arrangement of pebbles can be made to look like jewels.

'WHEN I HAVE A PIECE OF WOOD, I LOOK AT IT AND THINK ABOUT HOW I CAN TAKE IT FURTHER.'

ZOE RUMEAU

FANTASTIC BEASTS

Ferry van Tongeren, Haarlem, The Netherlands

The Dutch taxidermy company Darwin, Sinke & van Tongeren transforms nature's most beautiful designs and reinvents them into one-of-a-kind works of art. Driven by a love and respect for the natural world, their flamboyant, baroque-inspired taxidermy gives immortality at a time when so many species are endangered. In co-founder Ferry van Tongeren's home in Haarlem, three-dimensional masterpieces are on display, including a work comprising a 5.5 m (18 ft)-long king python, entwined with smaller snakes, and compositions that reinterpret Old Master paintings. Outside of the workshop, home is where Ferry gets to spend more time with his animals and behold the wonder of nature from his living room.

Taxidermy features throughout this modern-day version of a country house. In the hallway, Tom Dixon-designed black pendant lights coordinate with classic chequered tiles. A photograph by Ferry's company DSvT called *Réunion d'oiseaux étrangers* hangs on the bright yellow wall.

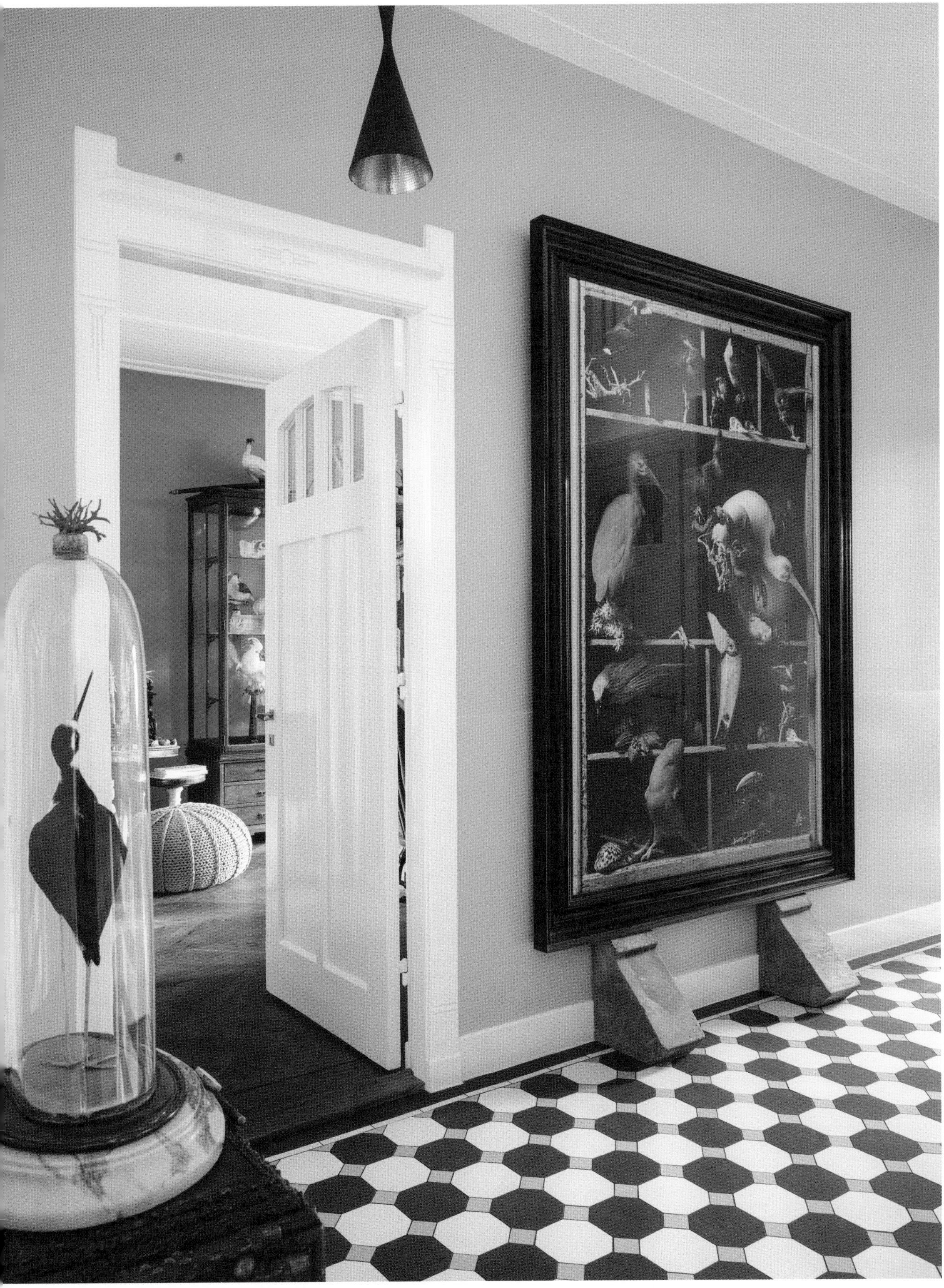

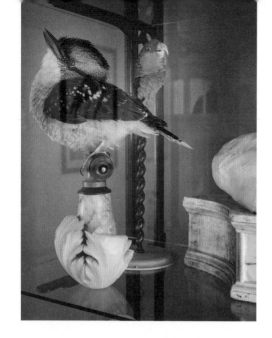

'IT IS IMPORTANT FOR US TO COLLECT AND BUY THESE
ANIMALS, BECAUSE THE ALTERNATIVE IS THAT THEIR BODIES
WOULD BE THROWN AWAY ONCE THEY DIED.'

In the blue-painted study, Ferry's collection of curiosities includes a snowy owl and a kookaburra. The bold colour scheme is far removed from the stuffy country-house aesthetic and contrasts with the vintage furniture. 'A lot of the stuff we collect is often brown, so we need bright colours on the wall,' Ferry says. 'I love colour very much.'

When Damien Hirst buys the entire contents of your first exhibition, you know that things are on track. Turning his back on a successful career in advertising, Ferry van Tongeren retrained as a taxidermist after a global gap-year adventure with his family, satisfying a lifelong interest in natural history. Having learned his craft under the wing of a leading Dutch taxidermist, he founded Darwin, Sinke & van Tongeren with friend and former colleague Jaap Sinke.

As skilled artists and taxidermists, the duo use their experience to capture the beauty and splendour of animals for eternity, and Ferry – along with his wife Marielle, who runs an antiques business – scours auctions and fairs for marble plinths and other ornaments to give their compositions authenticity and fun. Conjuring up stories inspired by 17th-century artists like Rubens and Melchior d'Hondecoeter, who painted newly discovered birds and animals brought to Europe for the first time, Ferry and Jaap place their creatures in dramatic poses that would have not have occurred naturally in the wild.

The provenance of the birds and animals they mount is extremely important, and they are all ethically sourced. 'Nowadays, the focus in zoos has changed from showing as many animals as possible to preserving rare and endangered species in breeding programmes,' Ferry explains. 'When you visit zoos, you are seeing the rarest creatures on earth. For us, it is important to collect and buy these animals, because the alternative is that their bodies would be thrown away once they died.'

In Ferry's 19th-century, punchy-painted home in Haarlem, the interior serves as a test bed for experiencing his exotic menagerie close up. Originally, animals were mounted as a scientific tool for naturalists to study. The same happens here. Ferry is aware of the tiniest detail of how an animal should look and is equally fascinated by the anatomy, which stems from his love of Renaissance art.

While on a walk as a child, Ferry happened upon a rabbit skull. 'I was blown away by its beauty, and the fact that I could take it home and own it for the rest of my life,' he says. 'I could also see how the rabbit looked when it was alive. I was already in love with nature. I did a lot of bird-watching with a pair of binoculars my grandfather gave me, but after I found that skull, I left the binoculars at home. I was only looking at the ground, instead of the sky. I started collecting, and inherited a collection from my grandfather, which forms the basis of everything I do now. I collected until puberty, but then drifted away. I thought it was childish and had more fun smoking. Later, when I was an adult, it started up again.'

In fact, it was a trip to Borneo that rekindled Ferry's passion and brought it full circle. After selling his advertising company, Ferry, Marielle and their two children took a year out to go travelling across Indonesia and Australasia. 'We bought a one-way ticket to Malaysia,' he says of the trip, which was intended to help him unwind from twenty-five years of advertising. 'I went travelling with the idea that I was retired, but had all sorts of business ideas that I just couldn't help thinking about. I told my wife that I was curious about learning how to do taxidermy. She thought it was meant as a hobby, and I thought the same. I never imagined it would turn into what it has become today.'

While in Borneo, Ferry was struck by the number of palm-tree plantations and the devastating effect of jungle deforestation not only on the landscape, but also on the habitats of the animals that lived there. 'There was so much roadkill,' he recalls. 'Civet cats, very big lizards and monkeys, all of whom were fleeing from this palm-tree shit going on and looking for a new place to live.' He started to photograph the lost souls wherever they travelled. Coming from a place of preservation, it was this reportage that triggered the idea of turning taxidermy into a business.

A photograph of a blue-and-yellow macaw posed in a milky soap water-bath is displayed along with other treasures. Ferry and Jaap use antique glass domes to use for showcase their work.

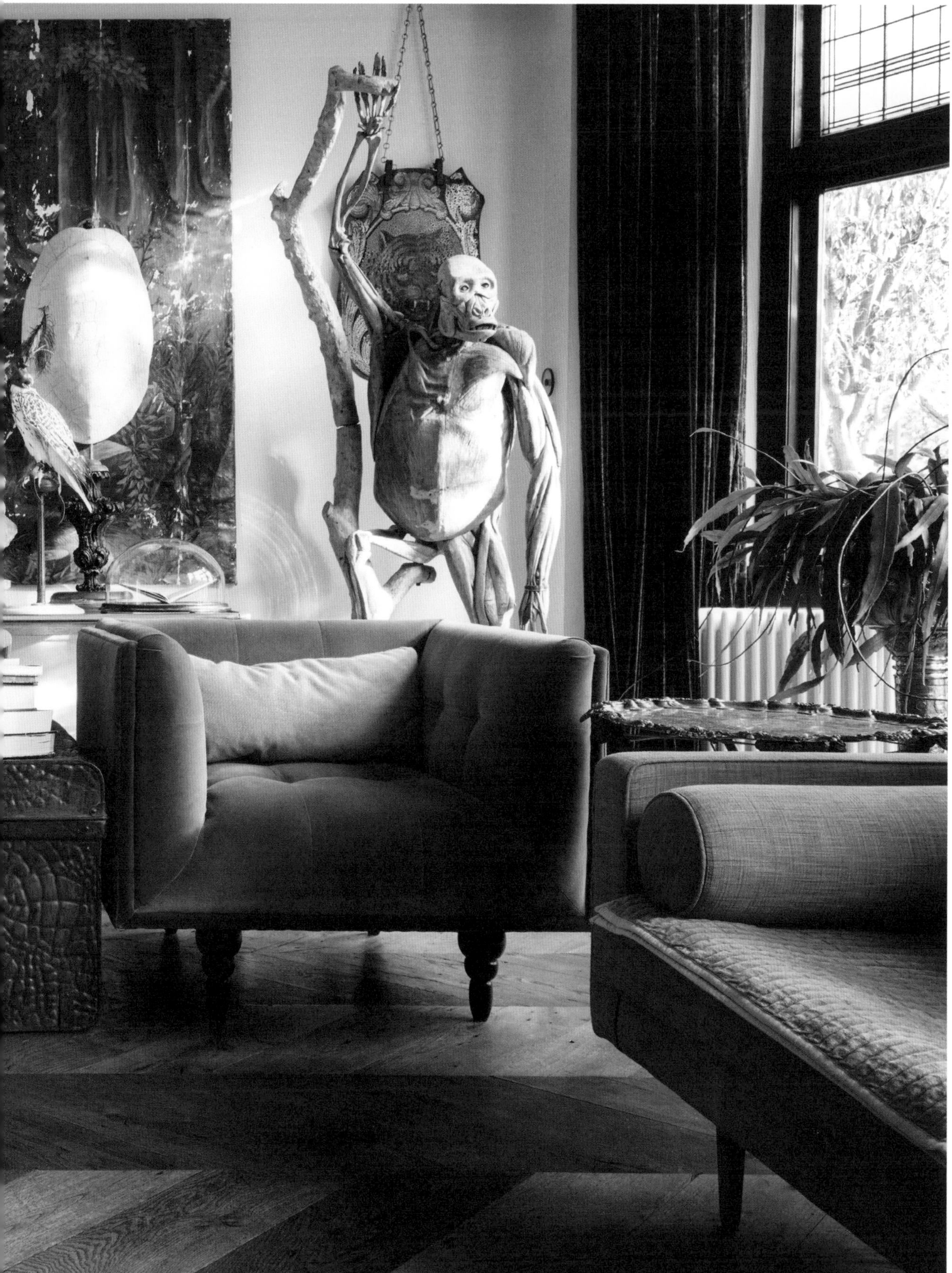

Painted a dark and moody charcoal grey, the master bedroom features skeletons of two different species of tamarin monkeys in glass cabinets, inspired by the drawings of the Comte de Buffon, a French naturalist. Downstairs in the dining room, a mounted zebra head hangs on the wall above the table.

1 To add drama to a collection, use a bright background to set it off. The sky-blue walls in my study emphasize the objects on display.

2 Look to art history for composition and colour reference. Dutch 17th-century paintings and art from the Italian Renaissance are starting points for my home and work.

3 What makes you smile? When grouping objects or choosing a palette, go with what you love.

4 For a period home filled with antique furniture, avoid an overload of brown by painting the walls in a bright colour. The room height can take it. There's no fussiness here – just more exuberance.

5 Look to nature as your guide. If it works on the feathers of a tropical bird, it will work in an interior.

FERRY VAN TONGEREN

'I WAS BLOWN AWAY BY THE BEAUTY OF THE RABBIT SKULL, AND THE FACT THAT I COULD TAKE IT HOME AND OWN IT FOR THE REST OF MY LIFE.'

BEACHCOMBERS

LADY BIRDS AND INSPIRATION FROM THE OCEAN
Kevin Beer, Los Angeles, USA

Beachy and rococo, the living room in this 1920s old Hollywood home is decorated with ornamental shells, coral sculptures and costumed bird creatures. In the hearth, pink-hued scallops and starfish are piled high in a giant South Pacific clam. A vintage chandelier hangs from the ceiling, adorned with lobster red-painted branches and teardrop sun-on-sea glass. Here, treasures from the ocean, found or crafted, have come together to create a fantastical home in the realm of reverie.

On the mantelpiece, a bust of Hadrian sits with coral sculptures and marine-shaped plants. It is the focal point of the room and sets the subterranean theme. The shells filling the large clam in the hearth have been collected over the years, sourced from flea markets or scouring the beach.

In the living room, Kevin covered the lintels above the doorway and windows with shellwork for decorative effect. The 1920s chandelier is also adorned with odd crystals, rosary beads, coral and painted branches. 'I treat it like a table centrepiece,' he says. 'It's always changing.'

Kevin Beer knows how to make an impression. The Texan-born interior designer, *coquillage* artisan and lover of the golden age of cinema understands the power of setting a scene. His home is an extension of his romantic, witty, engaging style – casually dapper and wonderfully eccentric. This sensibility has shaped the decor of his house, where he revels in narrative, playing around with colour while making miniature set designs and hybrid chimaera creatures in the studio. You could call him a magpie given how much he likes to collect. Hollywood is where he's made his nest, layered with art and antiques, toys and treasures – a colourful paean to a sentimental life and all things that inspire.

Kevin is a natural-born collector, and here in his home, nature is the focus. Shells are a thing, as seen in the scallop-backed chairs; mother-of-pearl decoration, blue glassware and birds also feature throughout. With items that range from garden-hose heads to love letters from the First and Second World Wars, it is Kevin's collection of doll's heads that is most unusual. Displayed in a glass-fronted cabinet to eerie effect, he uses them to concoct his magical miniatures, which are popular with film producers and art directors in LA. What makes them so special is the serendipity of finding them. 'I never take the doll's head off the doll, which also makes them so much harder to find,' he says. 'Each head has an individual face that over time, age and environment gets altered. To me, it makes them all the more interesting.'

As well as the dolls, there are butterflies and moths, which Kevin uses to create and adorn all types of things. In the living room, they are pinned to a painted portrait to cover damage caused by a workman's ladder. 'I collect insects for my work,' he explains. 'It all goes back to my childhood, I was always outside collecting and exploring. It's all about nature with me. The gardens, the animals, the forms, colours and scale – all of these things. I can't get enough.'

As a former antiques dealer, the act of collecting, keeping and preserving objects runs in Kevin's veins. In his home, vintage furniture is part of deal. 'Here, almost everything is family stuff I've inherited, from my parents to my great-great grandparents,' he notes. 'I have this Southern sensibility that if you inherit something, you keep it forever. That's why I have so many antiques.' Referring to his lushly planted garden, he says, 'I've been going through a floral period since my parents died. I'm sentimental. History is important to me – my personal history, especially. My parents and grandparents were dedicated gardeners. Flowers were everywhere.'

Yet alongside the antiques, there is a freshness to the decor, mostly to do with the striking colour palette of white and pale sky blue with aqua tints. 'I hate to use the phrase "light and airy", but it is,' Kevin says. His affection for the colour blue, as well as the use of shells to decorate the walls and encrust items of furniture, is what makes his house spirited, while still in context with its surroundings. 'You can't help being influenced by seashells when you live by the beach,' he adds. In the living room, he created the shellwork lintels above the windows and doorways, as well as the mermaid-ready, shell-framed mirror in the bathroom. The result is a deeply personal home.

'On the outside, I see my house as an old fishing shack in Mexico,' he says of the vivid tropical-island colours and casual vibe. 'The influence for me has always been the Gulf Coast, as well as the coastal communities of California.' As an art major, Kevin claims he can do a whole room around the inspiration of a painting by Gauguin. It's also no surprise that Louise Bourgeois is in his top ten. When asked who his house would be if it was a person, he offers: 'If Federico Fellini and Diane Arbus had a child.'

In the 1960s bathroom, a pair of vintage shellwork vases are paired with a homemade mirror. 'I'm always using seashells to cover pieces of furniture,' Kevin says. 'Many years ago, I bought boxes and boxes of broken coral and have been using them to make things ever since.' He dyes some of the coral to get the colour just how he likes it.

1 To contain pools of water, start with a good liner that will hold the water without cracking. Being watertight is super-important.

2 Use concrete to build a wall around the pool, adding shells and coral as you go. Try not to overthink placement.

3 Try placing a clam shell at the front of the pool for birds to bathe in the shallow water.

4 Choose plants that will hang nicely. The definition of a grotto is 'cavern', so vine-like plants will add to the effect.

5 A water feature is central. It is pretty to look at, and the running water will help mask traffic noise. You can also use it for rooting plant cuttings, or for floating flowers during a party. A family of raccoons love to bathe in mine.

6 Historic gardens and old churches are good reference points for design ideas. Just Google 'Italian grottoes', and you'll be inspired by what you find.

'YOU CAN'T HELP BEING INFLUENCED BY SEASHELLS
IF YOU LIVE BY THE BEACH.'

SHELL MAN
Thomas Boog, Poitiers, France

There is a house in the Vienne region in France that is unlike any other. It is the home of Swiss-born shell artist Thomas Boog, whose wizardry with *coquillage* brings together the many thousands of shells he buys in bulk from all over the world. Some are small and simple, used on repeat. The pattern and flow of these gathered shells are used to populate walls in place of wallpaper, or employed as jewels on a chandelier. Other, more fanciful specimens are used to conceive characterful wall sconces and marine masques. They're such happy objects: artistic, charismatic, handmade and unique. Far from a nautical-themed villa by the sea, this shell-filled home harks back to the tradition of wealthy travellers in the 17th and 18th centuries, bringing back their finds, and proves that shells are for the countryside, not just the beach.

Colour plays a strong role in the living room: red-lacquered chairs and turquoise-painted walls deliver on drama and complement the glass-fronted cabinets that house Thomas's white coral collection. These modern-day cabinets of curiosities were custom-made for the house, and painted black to avoid a beach-house vibe.

'I'm always using seashells to cover things,' Thomas says of the encrusted chandelier in the dining room and the cabinet covered with razor clams. 'I use clams as a precious material. The colours go from ivory to gold, almost like bamboo, but I think this looks more modern.'

There is a primal instinct behind collecting shells – or little branches, acorns or crystals – with the intention of using them to make something else. For shoe designer-turned-artist Thomas Boog, his shell-encrusted creations are the continuation of an old tradition. These are not beach souvenirs, but high-end interior design that includes the octopus-like chandelier at the Philippe Starck-designed SLS South Beach hotel in Miami and a modern grotto featuring a mother-of-pearl ceiling at the Royal Monceau hotel in Paris.

Thomas's side of the collector coin is defined by quantity, rather than a scientific 'one of each'. If you consider an architectural project, a tremendous number of shells is required. This means buying by the kilo, as well as plenty of sorting and searching for the right shell to fit the right space. 'That's what makes it so interesting,' he says. 'I'm not a scientist. To be a collector of that sort would mean entering a world that is a nightmare for me. My passion is for the beauty of shells. They are gifts from nature, and I want to make something with them.'

This, for Thomas, is far more fun than classifying the slightest degree of difference. He prefers to turn shells into an experience. Transferring his skills as a shoe designer to cobbling shells – Thomas was head of design at the Italian shoe brand Bally throughout the 1980s and early '90s – he thinks of them as a material. 'Shoes are a great complexity,' he explains. 'If you are good with shoes, you can design anything.'

Falling for the shell-decorated grottoes of Italy and wishing to recreate them at home, Thomas brings the beach to the country and turns fashion into craft. Starfish mirrors are a leitmotif. He likes the shape. 'Not the "real" starfish though,' he is keen to point out. 'You can't avoid the smell.' His favourite shell is *Turbo sarmaticus*, found off the coast of South Africa, for the mix of colours with bright mother-of-pearl. His collections often come from people who give him their own. 'They don't know what to do with them,' he says. 'This is the point.'

His keepsakes are the curiosities – the too big, the too small, the mistakes – which are stashed in a pair of custom-made glass-fronted cabinets in the living room. The examples kept here are the rare and unusual ones. 'If you take a razor clam for instance, the length is straight, but the width is curved,' Thomas explains. 'One shell in a million is curved along the length, too. It's a freak of nature. When I find one like that, it's like winning the lottery. It's very rare.' These, he puts aside. 'I've worked for thirty years in shells, and have found only two.'

For Thomas, shells have always been a point of reference in his life. Growing up in the mountains of Switzerland, a summer vacation to the beach was an exceptional thing – and proved particularly significant when illness prevented him from swimming in the sea one year. 'I was obliged to stay on my lounge chair,' he says. 'At that time, I looked more closely at shells. It was my only activity. I had all day to study and draw them, more so than the other girls and boys on the beach.'

He also recalls how his grandfather was able to make miracles out of nothing, gathering sticks and leaves from the Swiss mountain paths to build tiny little chalets without using glue. His outtake from this was that it is possible to create items of beauty with very little. 'That's the message,' he says. 'You can collect shells and they don't cost a thing, yet you can make something incredible. If you want to influence children and lead them towards an appreciation of art and nature, don't take them to a museum. It's too much. Instead, keep it simple – like my grandfather did.'

Thomas's office is next to the larger studio in one of the outbuildings on the estate. Covering an entire wall is a cabinet with wooden drawers, each marked with a shell making it easy to remember what's inside. 'I like a basketful of shells,' he says. 'The quantity makes it interesting. It turns the shells into a material you can do something with.'

'YOU CAN COLLECT SHELLS AND THEY
DON'T COST A THING, YET YOU CAN MAKE
SOMETHING INCREDIBLE.'

Thomas has thousands of shells in his house, which he uses to cover walls and items of furniture. Above the bath, he has meticulously lined up shells into a pattern resembling a Brunschwig & Fils wallpaper design. The wall sconce, which employs white shells and coral, is one of his bestsellers.

THOMAS'S TIPS FOR DECORATING WITH SHELLS FOR A COUNTRY HOUSE

1 Start with colours: once the colour choice is made, everything else will find its place.

2 For a modern look, stick to a single colour. Small shells in white look spectacular and work well in a contemporary scheme.

3 Try not to feel confined to the idea that shells are only for a beach house. This is the opposite of what people thought in the 18th century. Shell finds were always brought into the home.

4 To avoid an overly beachy feel, paint cabinets and coffee tables black.

5 Mix old and new, precious with less precious. It makes a period home feel less like a museum.

6 To create patterns, select the same size and colour of shell, such as a small and simple *Umbonium costatum*.

7 For any creation, don't start with beautiful shells. These are enough on their own, and are difficult to use in any composition.

8 Making Christmas decorations for the home is a nice way to bring children into the mix. Beautiful items can be made with little fingers.

'I'M NOT A SCIENTIST. TO BE A COLLECTOR OF THAT SORT WOULD MEAN ENTERING A WORLD THAT IS A NIGHTMARE FOR ME.'

THOMAS BOOG

THE STUFF OF SHELL DREAMS
Blott Kerr-Wilson, Norfolk, UK

Of all of nature's creations, shells have had a longstanding fascination for artists because of the beauty of their forms, colours and markings, as well as their evocation of voyages and the magic of the underworld. In Europe, a craze for shells sprang up in the 16th century, with wealthy landowners chartering ships to the New World to bring back items of curiosity. Today, the collections of modern shell hounds aren't sitting pretty, gathering dust on shelves, but are used for their work or kept as 'shell postcards', serving as memories of the places they came from. Artist Blott Kerr-Wilson first became intrigued by shells after visiting the gardens of stately homes in her youth. Now, her exquisite murals and shell-house commissions are as luminous, beguiling and opulent as the shells themselves.

'When I first started, I would only use British shells,' Blott says, 'because I didn't have any money and could get them for free. As time went on, the world of shells and of buying them absolutely opened up to me. I didn't have a clue that there were all these different varieties available.'

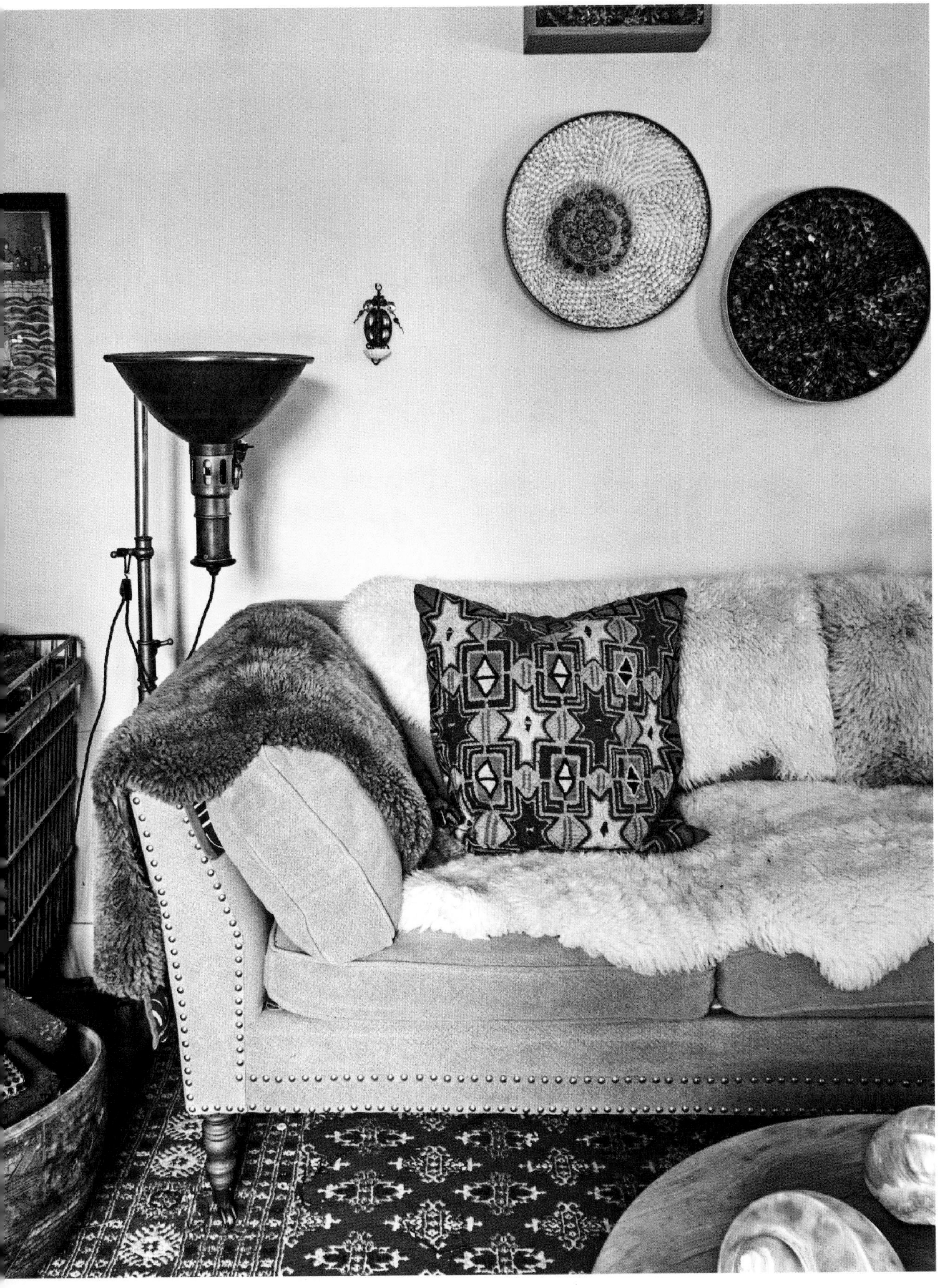

Blott's obsession with collecting spills over beyond shells into textiles and art. The portrait above the fireplace is of her mother in Paris, while the tapestry cushions on the sofa were made by a friend. 'I absolutely love them,' she says. 'I don't buy one, I buy five. I do things en masse.'

'IT'S THE ONE THAT GETS PUT ON THE COMPOST HEAP – NOBODY NOTICES IT – YET IT IS THE ONLY BLUE SHELL THAT EXISTS IN NATURE.'

Blott Kerr-Wilson describes her work as making tapestries with shells. 'I create stories for myself,' she says. 'Each piece is emotional, and whatever is going on in my life at that time goes into it. Sometimes when I look back at a work, it's really tight, because there was a lot going on in my head at the time. And then there are much calmer, more peaceful ones, like the one in my studio.' Blott is referring to the elaborate yet beautifully restrained mural on her easel, due shortly to wing its way to a client in New York. Using only *Haliotis asinina*, the mother-of-pearl interiors of the shells catch the light, owing to the murmuration movement she has cleverly whipped into shape.

Blott's purpose-built studio next to the house is a like a sweet shop, where the walls are stacked not with sherbet lemons, but with shells. And don't be fooled by the organization of the glass jars. 'There is no order in nature,' she insists of the dolly mixtures of shells within. 'I have them arranged in the jars because I find the results incredibly beautiful. I like to surprise myself with a shell I've forgotten about and start it using again.'

She gathers and she makes. Whether it is her shell collection or the many other bird- and sea-related items amassed in her home, things don't come and go, they get added to. Textiles, lights and paintings made by friends are both objects of beauty and revealing of personal journeys. 'They are all connections with people and memories from jobs,' Blott says. 'I like to surround myself with things that make me smile.'

Born in Wales, Blott was sent to boarding school in England at the age of eight. 'I had this very strange upbringing,' she says. 'We didn't really spend any time with my parents. My sister and I were feral, but the one thing we did do was go and visit gardens. They are so boring when you're little, but I saw the shell houses and grottoes and it stuck with me. When I moved into my council flat in Peckham, where I thought I would live forever more, I made a shell room.' That was her first, and the one that won a competition in *World of Interiors* magazine in 1993.

Since then, Blott has been a thriving artist, living for twenty years in France near La Rochelle. She now lives on the north Norfolk coast, cold-water swimming in the sea, and is a trustee of the Glandford Shell Museum, a couple of fields away. She is in a place where she is truly meant to be. Her pretty painted bungalow, with its French-style shutters, is in sync with the landscape, the pink matching the wheat fields at certain times of the year. Inside, the interior is packed with handmade textiles and art, including some of Blott's own pieces, made from cowrie and mussel shells.

'This is the shell I love the most,' she says of the mussel. 'It's the one that gets put on the compost heap – nobody notices it – yet it is the only blue shell that exists in nature. There are loads of different mussels, including a pheasant shell with a turquoise inside – it really does look like a feather.'

Blott is drawn to shells for their beauty and the incredible ways in which they can be used. Their attraction extends to how shells like the cowrie have been used by native peoples in embroidery, as well as for currency. 'I have a respect for the cowrie, because it's got this incredible history,' she says, 'when you think that tribes used it who weren't even close to the sea. It's just extraordinary how a shell can have that power.'

In the kitchen, there is a mishmash of possessions, from Welsh tea towels to collected eggs, shoe trees with phone chargers hanging off them and tropical Murex shells. Of these, she says, 'I'm not a fan of the spikes or the pink inside. They are a bit Barbara Cartland for me.'

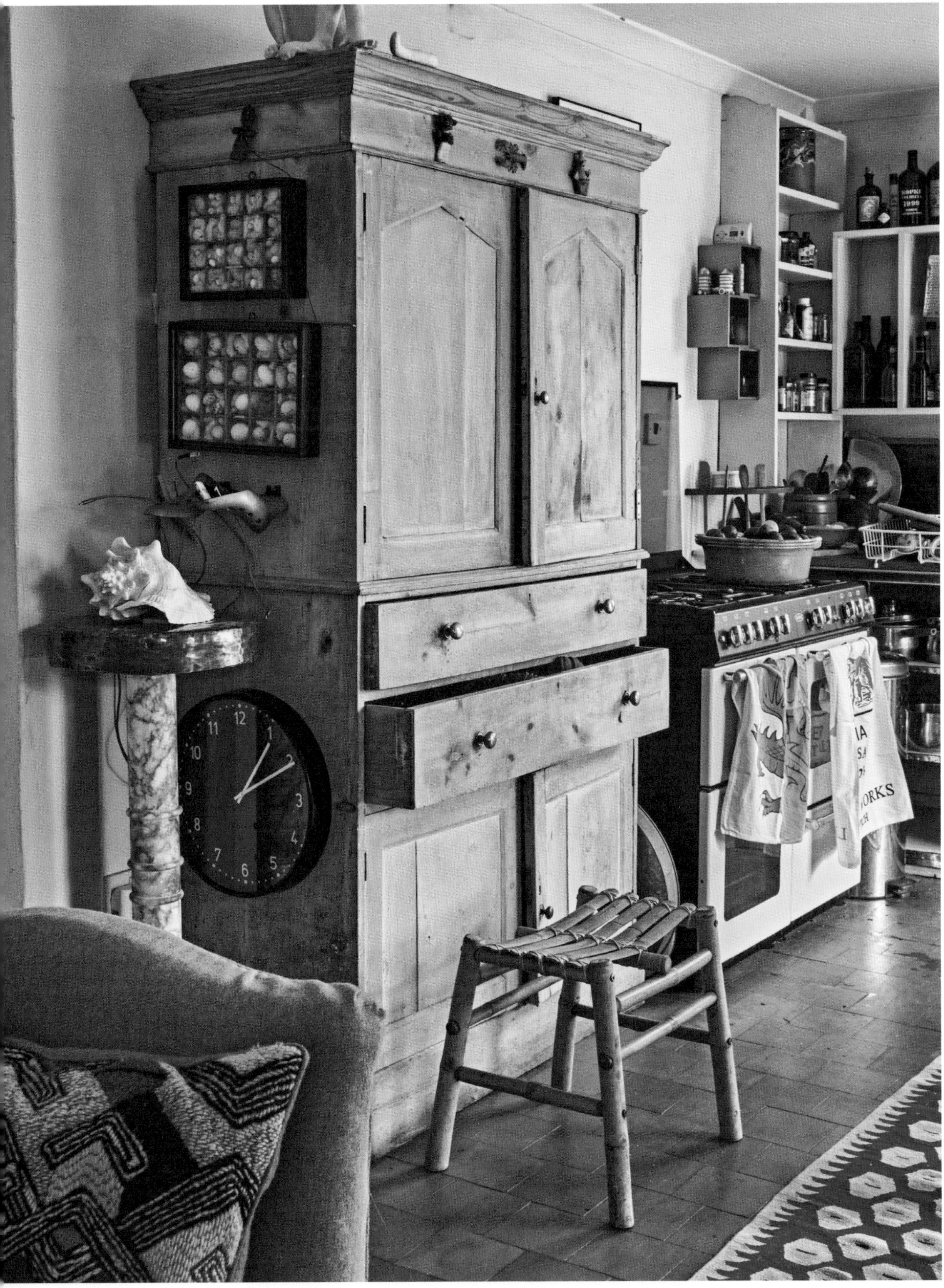

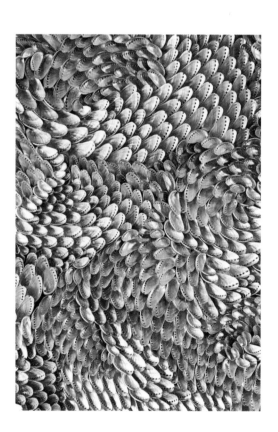

'I HAVE THE SHELLS ARRANGED IN JARS BECAUSE
I FIND THE RESULTS INCREDIBLY BEAUTIFUL.'

Blott spends a lot of her time sorting, arranging and rejecting shells, as each one is different yet so similar. Whereas a painter has control over their own work, each time Blott places a shell, she has to adjust and readjust it to fit the next. The shells take the lead.

A visit to Blott's house is also a pilgrimage to the bijoux shell museum in Glandford, only two fields away. It is the sweetest home to one of the finest seashell collections in the UK, of which Blott is a trustee.

BLOTT'S
TIPS FOR
USING SHELL
ARTWORK

1 Believe in yourself, and have patience. Every piece of work goes through an ugly stage – you just have to work through it. The likelihood is that you will come out of it and be proud of what you have done.

2 Use the shells that you find and that you want to use. Play around with them and be free.

3 Create a frame and work within it. If you don't, you won't have any borders and that's really scary.

4 Try not to leave any cement showing around the shells. This means that you will need to go slowly. Work on a small area at a time.

5 If the finished piece is to go on a wall, try to create it standing upright, rather than lying flat. This way, you can see how the light will look on the shells.

6 Start anywhere but in the middle, unless you are creating a spiral.

'I LIKE TO SURROUND MYSELF WITH THINGS
THAT MAKE ME SMILE.'

SHELL SEEKER
Luca Zanaroli, Puglia, Italy

From Henry Moore to Barbara Hepworth, the sea and all its offerings have been a source of wonder for artists and collectors throughout the years. This architect-homeowner, now based in Bologna, has lived in rural Puglia in southern Italy since he was a child. He draws deeply from the coastline's natural beauty when he returns to the region for visits to his holiday home, a modern three-bedroom villa where the interiors are decorated with collected shells, sea urchins and starfish, all arranged with an artist's eye.

Describing himself as a 'finder and keeper', Luca has styled his beach house simply, so as not to interfere with the sea view. Natural materials lead the decor, and furniture is kept low and boxy. The artwork in the living room was created by gathering wood offcuts left over from the outdoor terrace.

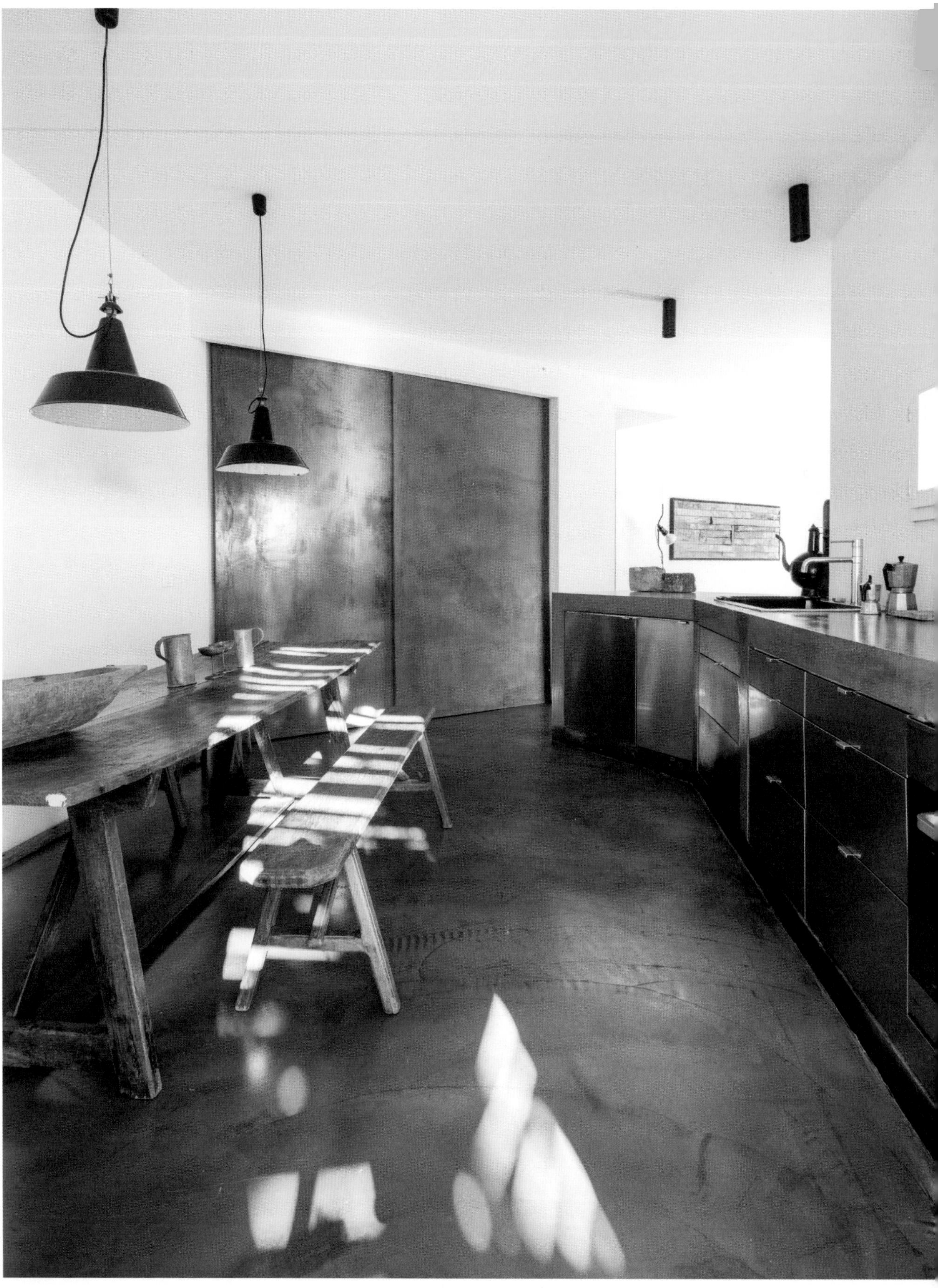

'WHAT COMES FROM NATURE, PARTICULARLY
FROM THE SEA, REPRESENTS WHAT I CONSIDER
TO BE PERFECT/IMPERFECT.'

'I love to collect anything that attracts me, whether because of its shape or the material it is made from,' says Luca Zanaroli. He is fascinated by the shapes found in nature, and his studies both spark his imagination and inform his work. Standing in two-and-a-half acres of outstanding natural beauty, his holiday home has been designed with materials that blend into the landscape, including stone for the cladding that Luca found in the grounds. 'What comes from nature, particularly from the sea, represents what I consider to be perfect/imperfect,' he adds.

As a child, Luca would spend his school holidays in the region, and feels a strong connection to it. His enthusiasm for the location and its washed-up components is part of the lifestyle this home in Puglia offers. Every summer, Luca goes to the seashore and a new shape of shell or pebble will catch his eye, which will then appear on his table or on the walls. 'I love the sea and I love walking on the shore in search of what has washed up,' he says. 'I always wanted to have somewhere by the sea that I could keep the things I found on my walks. The house is the realization of this desire.'

Luca is the child of foragers, and it was his mother who passed on to him a passion for finding things left on the beach. 'I spent hours with her as a child,' he remembers, 'strolling along the shore in search of everything that would intrigue me. I have always kept the objects that fascinated me, but I am not a true collector, more of a finder and keeper. I like the unique things I find along the way, and I like to keep the memory of this special moment. After all, it's like the random encounters that take place throughout one's life. In some way, you try to keep the memory of it.'

In his home, Luca has used mostly natural materials and found objects from antiques markets, as well as making many items himself with recycled materials, often found in nearby fields. He likes things that are alive with the flavour of nature and sea air. 'I have always liked the idea of using objects that had a different function originally from the one I give them in my furnishings,' he explains. 'In addition to turning a drinking trough into a sink, I used an old gate as a headboard for a bed and skeins of rusted iron as a chandelier.'

The beach house is well stocked with objects, both refined and raw. 'I consider my collections as compositions of things that together create an aesthetically complete and evocative image,' he says. 'In the arrangement of shells on the wall, each box contains the idea of the seashore – the time and the place – where the shells were collected. Visitors to Puglia should head straight to the beach, the coastline here is fantastic.'

'EACH BOX CONTAINS THE IDEA OF THE SEASHORE – THE TIME AND THE PLACE – WHERE THE SHELLS WERE COLLECTED.'

Luca and his wife Silvia spend their holidays foraging for treasures that can be used in the house. In the cement-floored kitchen, hollowed-out tree trunks have been filled with traditional farming tools for decorative effect.

Luca displays his collections of shells in simple frames. The boxed installations are a simple way to organize and show items in quantity. 'I really like the skeleton of the sea urchin,' he says. 'It has such a strong yet light shape.'

In the bathroom, a stone trough has been repurposed as a wash basin. 'I like to reuse things in unexpected ways,' Luca says. 'I mix these reclaimed elements with vintage pieces that I pick up at flea markets.'

LUCA'S TIPS
FOR STYLING
ITEMS FORAGED
FROM THE SEA

1 Try a linear arrangement to draw the eye to individual shapes and materials. It can be something as simple as a plain white shelf holding the items you love most.

2 To highlight an object's precious quality, try placing it within a box frame or under a bell jar. As soon as something is presented behind or underneath glass, it becomes an art form.

3 For a neat and organized feel, group items according to type and colour.

4 Shells can be repurposed as items in the home. Larger ones can make platters and vases, whereas smaller shells like scallops look pretty when hung on a door or in a pattern on the wall.

5 Embrace the rustic nature of driftwood, using a large branch to hang a curtain or create a canopy above the bed.

'I ALWAYS WANTED TO HAVE SOMEWHERE BY THE SEA I COULD KEEP THE THINGS I FOUND ON MY WALKS. THE HOUSE IS THE REALIZATION OF THIS DESIRE.'

LUCA ZANAROLI

STORYTELLING
IN STONE

SAY IT WITH CRYSTALS
Carol Woolton, London, UK

Some people love flowers, others have a thing for rocks and create little altars to the things that fascinate them, collected over a lifetime. In the case of Carol Woolton – historian, stylist and jewelry editor of *British Vogue* – the magic of stones is her job, as well as her hobby. In her work, she tends to speak about highly polished, cut and faceted precious pieces, but at home she focuses on the natural form of stones, enthralled by the combination of geometry, geology and spiritual properties that have accrued over time. Not only are stones deeply reassuring in their sense of permanence, reminding you that the earth has always been there, but they are also utterly beautiful. Like an eternal version of a floral bouquet, the natural force of a stunning crystal will uplift and transfix.

In the drawing room, light floods through a large citrine stone, bought from crystal and fossil specialist Dale Rogers. The colour complements Carol's peach-coloured swag curtains, and brings a positive, life-affirming energy to the space. The bronze and white enamel chandelier was commissioned from Yunus & Eliza, who also made the jewelry for *Games of Thrones*.

On the coffee table is a large black quartz from Brazil, also bought from Dale Rogers, paired with a blue celestite cluster from Peter Adler *(see pp. 106–15)*. Carol treats her mantelpieces as mini-cabinets of curiosities, where geodes sit alongside personal treasures, including a letter from Marc Jacobs and photos from *Vogue* shoots that Carol has worked on.

When we speak of the personality and character in interiors, it is usually linked to the personal objects that mean something to the homeowner living there. In the drawing room of this elegant property in south London, a branch from the garden was cast in bronze to create a bespoke chandelier, and in the conservatory, a mural of silver birch trees brings the outdoors in. Crystals are all around. Flowers, trees and stones – a trilogy of nature in decorative form.

'I see lots of similarities between flowers and my love of stones,' Carol says of her exquisite crystal collection. 'They are both natural phenomena, are rooted in the earth and share a sort of magic that brings primal emotions of wonder, desire and greed in some circumstances. Through various periods in history, hunters have risked their lives to acquire both, whether a beautiful stone or an exotic orchid. If you're not very green-fingered, which I have to admit I'm not, it's good to have something alive in the room. If you can't have fresh flowers around the whole time, having a big crystal does the same job.'

Specific stones are sited in certain places around the house, from the unusually large golden citrine in the drawing room, which co-ords perfectly with the swag curtains, to the amethyst geode Carol discovered in the garden when she first moved in. 'It was extra-ordinary,' she says. 'When I first saw this house, I had a physical reaction to it. I had an overarching sense that this would be my home, and that I would live there. My husband and I moved in, and about two days later I kicked something in the garden. It was the geode. Somebody must have put it there at some point, but I thought – doing what I do, collecting what I collect – this is what I found. I keep half outside and the other half inside.'

Tastes may change, but once a collector, always a collector. During her childhood, Carol recalls, she collected items from pieces of Carltonware china to vintage scent bottles, which she would pick up cheaply at junk stores.

Drawn like a magpie to anything a bit sparkly, she remembers buying a lump of rose quartz – a stone she still loves today. 'My big pink Madagascar quartz on the kitchen mantelpiece was my first major purchase,' she says. 'I had to have it. It is difficult to explain. When you see a stone, there's something extraordinary about it, almost a primeval magic that it has been extracted from the earth. You have that direct connection to how it's meant to be.'

Carol was influenced by her father, a stockbroker who specialized in diamonds and stones. He would often return from his travels with small stones for his daughter, such as a tiger's eye from South Africa. She also spent her formative years living in Australia and recalls receiving a small opal as a bridesmaid's gift, which she still has today. 'I remember coming back from Australia via Hong Kong, where you could buy precious pieces of jade in tiny silk pouches. It all seemed so sophisticated and magical to me.'

She has since worked with stones and jewellers for decades, working at *British Vogue* for over twenty years and at *Tatler* before that, carving out the position of jewelry editor – a role that hadn't really existed before. Carol's book *The New Stone Age* (2020) is the culmination of her experience with and knowledge of stones, exploring a movement that is less LA-mystical, and more part scientific, part wellbeing, part art.

'Stones have a life within them,' she says. 'Jewellers would tell me they only cut rubies in the morning, otherwise they can't sleep at night as the stones are so full of fire and passion. They do sapphires after lunch.' A collector herself, she wanted to look a bit deeper into what this fascination actually meant and what the energetic value of it was, whether it is in the jewelry you wear or in the minerals on display on the mantelpiece. 'We are emulating the ancients,' she adds. 'This resonates with the younger generation, who are looking to make sure the earth is honoured. Stones are a reminder of the duty we have.'

'STONES HAVE A LIFE WITHIN THEM.'

Carol likes to bring flowers and trees into her home to display in combination with her crystals. The wallpaper in the bedroom is 'Richmond Park' by Zoffany, and in the dining room, the hand-painted silver birch mural is by artist Dawn Reader.

'I SEE LOTS OF SIMILARITIES BETWEEN FLOWERS
AND MY LOVE OF STONES.'

Carol keeps her collection of agates by the office door, both for their appearance and for their usefulness in keeping the door open. 'They've lived there for so long now that I know they like being there,' she says. *Overleaf* The totems of turquoise and rose quartz are by artist Celia Lindsell.

CAROL'S TIPS
FOR USING
CRYSTALS IN
THE HOME

1 Try placing a large crystal on a mantelpiece or coffee table instead of a vase of flowers. It's good to have something alive in the room to lift the spirits and add nature's colours. For me, they do the same job.

2 To start a collection, rock crystals are good, as the clear colour sits well in any home. The ancient Japanese called them the 'perfect jewel', because they symbolize space, purity and perseverance.

3 For an easy decorative effect, a bowlful of palm crystals look nice on a dressing table. I also have a smooth, round Labradorite pebble that I keep in my handbag. There's something irresistible and soothing about holding a stone in your hand.

4 Try placing rose quartz on the bedside table, so it is the last thing you look at before going to sleep. Many find the colour restful. I like a flicker of hopeful pink in the kitchen, as it is where we mostly congregate as a family. It sparks a positive reaction, and I imagine there's a gently balanced rhythm to its pink hues spreading throughout the house.

5 There are no rules when choosing a crystal. Just go with what you are drawn to, and trust your gut instinct. It's a personal choice, and our reactions to different colours can vary wildly. Have your own perception of the colour, rather than what it is meant to do.

'WHEN YOU SEE A STONE, THERE'S SOMETHING EXTRAORDINARY ABOUT IT, ALMOST A PRIMEVAL MAGIC THAT IT HAS BEEN EXTRACTED FROM THE EARTH.'

CAROL WOOLTON

A ROCK LOVER'S PARADISE

Peter Adler, London, UK

Many of us have notions of what a collector's home might be like. We imagine a serene, empty space that acts as a blank canvas for the display of important works of art, or a den of activity, full of treasures, which borders on hoarding. If you ask the collectors themselves about the role their home plays as a conduit for displaying their favourite things, there are all sorts of circumstance that come into play. It's not always about aesthetics, or surrounding yourself with foraged items you couldn't resist picking up from the beach. Take jeweller and antiques dealer Peter Adler, whose home is heavily ornamented with tribal-inspired jewelry and magnificent hunks of crystals in their natural form. By his own admission, stuff tends to pile up. But as well as a collector, Peter is a dealer, too. And as much as things accumulate, he is equally happy to let them go.

Objects in the living room are organized according to colour, so that each piece is easier to find when stylists come calling for props. The mix is part tribal, part Peter's own design. A pair of ceremonial hats from the Bamileke tribe in Cameroon make a glorious focal point.

The living room is crammed full with travel-triggered shells, fossils, stones, works of art and books. The assortment of carved sculptures includes a 19th-century Guanyin, a Buddhist deity from China, and a Luba Hemba figure from the Congo.

'I call it my tribute to minimalism,' says Peter of his fabulously cluttered home and studio in central London. 'Most people who visit say it's like an Aladdin's cave.' The connection is understandable. His home is a feast for the eyes wherever you look. With its brick red-painted walls and engaging variety of precious objects, gathered with a connoisseur's eye, it feels exactly like a mineral gallery in a natural-history museum, rather than a magnet for Marie Kondo types. But as a dealer and jeweller behind Pebble London, items do come and go – one day to furnish a Jurassic-themed film set at Pinewood Studios, or photographed for the pages of *Vogue* on the next.

Faceted and tumbled semiprecious stones, along with larger pieces of coral, amber and wonderful tribal art, form the basis of Peter's collection, accumulated as a consequence of his wanderlust. 'It's a wonderful excuse for travelling,' he admits. 'My collection started as an excuse to go to wonderful places, in particular India. That was the switch. I became fascinated by tribal culture, and especially by the craft, along with items from nature, such as fossilized giant clam shells, petrified wood and natural stones. When I was in India for the first time, it became more about how I could justify coming back.'

He is reminded of his tendency for collecting shells and little stones as a child growing up in California. 'We had a lovely neighbour in Beverly Hills who had the most magical collection of crystals and minerals and shells,' he recalls. 'I was like a kid in a candy shop. As a three- or four-year-old, I was entranced. To this day, I still love shells, as well as minerals, crystals and fossils. I love an explosion of colour.'

Peter began to buy amazing rocks and minerals on his travels in Africa and the Far East, or from fossil fairs, including his favourite in the Alsace, claiming that although technically he is a dealer, he buys as a collector. 'In other words,' he says, 'if nobody buys what I've bought, I'm perfectly happy with that. For me, it's nothing to do with fashion, or what's in or what's out. I buy what I like. I'm drawn to things for aesthetic reasons and by how something looks.'

His home is a breath of fresh air for anyone opposed to New Age crystal therapy. People who visit are free to choose the stones they want. 'It's all about gut instinct,' he says. There isn't a hint of nostalgia or sentimentality to his way of thinking. Peter firmly believes that it's fine to be seduced by glittery, shiny things; the mere fact that a stone gives pleasure is reason enough. His passion is for getting crystals out there for people to enjoy.

For the tribal-inspired jewelry that Peter creates for Pebble London, his philosophy is to avoid over-designing, buying stones that he thinks would work as a necklace, having them drilled and strung up. 'I love working with raw materials,' he says. 'I like to keep things as simple as possible, because what nature makes is so stunning. I don't try to improve on it.'

Despite this desire for simplicity, one look at this home creates entirely the opposite impression. Evidently, there is lots of 'simple' stuff. 'The result is from a lack of space,' he admits. 'In the living room, there really should be far less going on, but it builds up over time.' For Peter, it is impossible to deny the lure of minerals and stones. It is also impossible not to describe this home as an Aladdin's cave.

'TO THIS DAY, I STILL LOVE SHELLS,
AS WELL AS MINERALS, CRYSTALS AND FOSSILS.
I LOVE AN EXPLOSION OF COLOUR.'

Ammonites from the Jurassic period sit inside a giant clam shell from Kenya. The black ones are 'ammonite negatives', impressions left in the rock when the fossil is removed.

PETER ADLER

AFRICAN TWILIGHT

AFRICAN TWILIGHT 2

AFRICAN TWILIGHT 3

The large shard of transparent blue, sitting on a rough malachite boulder, is naturally occurring volcanic glass from Java. The glass has been polished, but keeps the original shape. 'You can't beat nature, that's my motto,' Peter says. In front are pieces of turquoise, jade and chrysocolla.

'I CALL IT MY TRIBUTE TO MINIMALISM.'

In the bedroom and bathroom, the mood is much more beachy, with a four-poster bed wrapped in muslin and a mother-of-pearl wall hanging, which Peter has threaded onto a twig. The doors open out onto the conservatory. A passionate gardener, Peter likes the jungle look.

PETER'S TIPS
FOR CHOOSING
A CRYSTAL
THAT'S RIGHT
FOR YOU

1 Don't focus too much on the healing properties of crystals or the zodiac. Instead, be free to choose one that you want. It's fine to be drawn to something purely because of the way it looks.

2 Try not to become overwhelmed by choice. I choose my crystals aesthetically. Visual impact and gut instinct are the very best guides.

3 Spend time looking at colours. One may glint more than others. Go with that.

4 Pick a stone up or try holding your hand over a range of colours to see what sensations you can pick up as your hand moves around.

5 For strength and healing powers, Labradorite from Madagascar is the king of crystals. It is possible to measure the energy waves that a stone produces, and Labradorite is off the charts. I'm a firm believer in its healing powers.

6 Once you take a crystal home, it is important to wash the stone to get rid of other people's energies.

'I LIKE TO KEEP THINGS AS SIMPLE AS POSSIBLE,
BECAUSE WHAT NATURE MAKES IS SO STUNNING.'

PETER ADLER

NEOLITHIC LOVE
Oliver Gustav, Copenhagen, Denmark

It's hard not to adore Oliver Gustav. He is the epitome of Danish good humour, open generosity and extraordinary taste, which inevitably extends to his home in Copenhagen. Intimate, organized and pulsating with his soul-satisfying collections, his private universe is where ancient Asian and Egyptian antiquities and found curiosities meet. Not everything is high status. It is a hedonistic set up that gives a glorious snapshot of this designer's peaceful yet spellbinding style, brought to life in this unique 1914 historic home – essentially a single-room space with a bedroom built in the loft. Surrounded by light, the house is a dream venue for showing off beautiful objects and works of art.

Oliver regularly visits auction houses across Europe to fill his home and shop. Items are in constant rotation, with certain pieces removed from time to time. He is keen to point out that the objects on display are definitely not to do with any kind of showing off. 'I only collect for myself,' he says. 'It has become my life to be surrounded by beautiful things.'

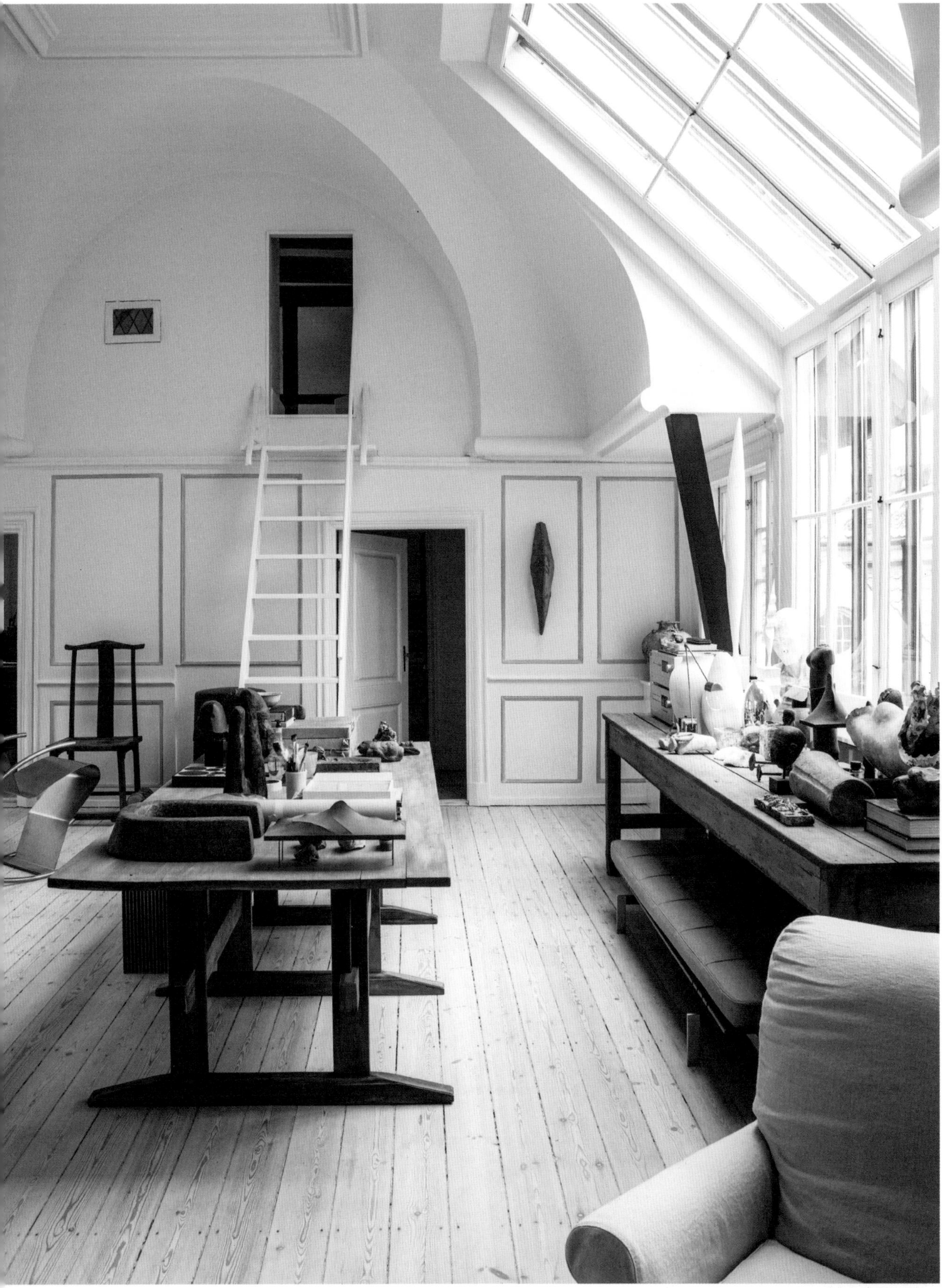

The loft serves as Oliver's primary residence and as a refuge from his busy life. In this dramatic, white-painted space, he has created a tension between ancient and modern. 'I tend to collect both high-tech furniture and natural items, as I love how they make each other stronger,' he says.

Sometimes you enter a room, and get a feel for the mood right away. You sense a little of the person who lives there, and if their style is chaotic, classy or carefree. In this nest-like home, there is more than a touch of the classy. It also delivers a massive punch of simplicity and harmony beneath the fabulous skylit roof. The interior is like a stage set, in which Oliver is surrounded by beautiful things – some precious in terms of monetary value, others whose worth is all to do with colour, texture and shape. 'It could be a simple piece of wood or a stone I found,' he says. 'It has its own value if it gives me joy.'

Oliver has a passion for honest and raw materials. On the centre table is a stone yoke from Veracruz, Mexico, which dates back to the 6th century, a zoomorphic figure from Papua New Guinea called the Ambum stone, and an ancient Egyptian stone sculpture of the female pharaoh Hatshepsut. All of these incredible vignettes from various moments in the world's history are not arranged according to theme. Oliver's personality jumps in too many different directions for that. When he comes across an interesting object that he feels the need to own, the trigger is love. It is serendipity.

Originally brought up in the rural outskirts of Copenhagen, Oliver divides his time between his home in the city and a summer house at the northern tip of Sealand. 'Nature and silence are important for me,' he says. 'I need both in my life. I could easily live in the countryside full time, but I don't think it would be healthy for me. I'm too young.' His daily routine involves going down to the pier each morning to dive into the water before his morning cup of tea. 'For me, it's the perfect way to be in the city and be in touch with the rawness of nature.'

Oliver's love of nature and collecting comes from his grandfather, a blacksmith, who himself had an eclectic eye. 'His father lived in China for almost thirty years in the early 20th century,' he explains. 'He was a huge collector of Asian and Egyptian antiquities. We never met, but my grandfather inherited a large part of that collection. Visiting my grandparents' house was always a very special thing. I was so attracted to that world of treasures and ancient pieces.'

Later in life, this passion was honed by the visionary set designer and furniture-maker Tage Andersen, known for his magical store in Copenhagen with its magnificent floral displays. Oliver worked with Tage for eight years, shortly after leaving home when he was eighteen. 'He was probably the most impossible man I ever met,' Oliver recalls. 'He taught me to work really hard. The years after being kicked out of the house were difficult years for me. I never got a full education, because I simply needed to survive. But I had a feeling, and somehow I made a living out of that.'

Anyone familiar with Oliver's showrooms in Copenhagen and New York, where he presents work by cutting-edge contemporary designers alongside 17th-century antiques and ancient sculpture, will know of his brilliance, as well as the conflict between his passion and profession. 'I had a reputation for having many beautiful pieces in my showroom and nothing was for sale,' Oliver admits. 'I would bring in pieces I didn't want to sell, simply because I wanted people to enjoy and appreciate them in the same way I do. Now it is easier. I'm better at not showing pieces that are not for sale.'

In his home, the skylights dominate the space. 'I was attracted to that,' he says of the building, a former private art gallery for a Dutch shipping magnate. 'Even though the rooms are large and the ceiling is high, the way the space wraps around you is very special.' Here, you are ensconced in Oliver's vision – his personal temple and love affair with living with stone.

'NATURE AND SILENCE ARE IMPORTANT FOR ME.
I NEED BOTH IN MY LIFE.'

'VISITING MY GRANDPARENTS' HOUSE WAS ALWAYS
A VERY SPECIAL THING. I WAS SO ATTRACTED TO THAT
WORLD OF TREASURES AND ANCIENT PIECES.'

The natural light filtering into the room brings a beauty to the objects on display. Walls are covered in linen and painted for added softness and a lovely acoustic quality.

1 For a space that feels calm, despite being surrounded by many items, I like to keep to a nude, or neutral, palette, so that nothing takes too much attention in the room.

2 Stick to natural and tactile materials – such as wood, clay and stone – for the interior scheme and the pieces on display.

3 To collect items with integrity, and that will mean something to you, think about the culture that produced them, as well as the material and shape.

4 Try beginning with symmetry when giving thought to the placement and scale of objects – and then break it.

5 Choose love. A collection doesn't need to have a monetary value for it to have worth.

'EVEN THOUGH THE ROOMS ARE LARGE
AND THE CEILING IS HIGH, THE WAY THE SPACE
WRAPS AROUND YOU IS VERY SPECIAL.'

ROCK STARS
Mark and Eloise Appel, Los Angeles, USA

From a sculpture created from a redwood tree from Big Sur in California to an agatized coral from Florida and a hunk of copper from Michigan, the most fundamental of elements are displayed in this architect-designed home in place of works of art. Rather than a Rothko or Hirst hanging on the wall, instead there is a giant fossilized fish plate from Wyoming, featuring a shrimp and a stingray, which dates back to the Eocene era, 55 million years ago. At the living-room window, a slice of agate allows the West Coast sunlight to shine through. Collecting rocks is a lifelong passion for Mark and Eloise Appel, rooted in knowledge and the astonishment of form, dismantling barriers between art and science. It is the stuff of life.

This contemporary home was designed by Mark and the couple's architect son, Brett Appel. Its simplicity showcases the objects on display as if they were museum exhibits. The large slice of translucent agate in the living room looks incredible with the light shining through. 'We're lucky as our house has so much light,' Mark says. 'It comes from every direction.'

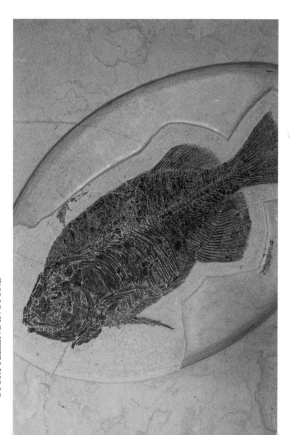

'THE COLOURS ARE MOSTLY EARTH TONES,
ALTHOUGH SOME GEMS ARE MORE COLOURFUL.
THERE IS A VARIETY.'

To describe this couple's close bond with stones would be an understatement. Drawn by shape, texture and a childlike intrigue, Mark and Eloise Appel's love affair with collecting items from the earth is a passion shared. One is a retired architect who spent his career using natural forms; the other had a business in educational evaluation, and by her own admission is probably the least artistic of the family. They come together over their interest in geology. They are much less inclined to decorate with or be drawn to paintings created by humans than they are by objects that come from the natural world.

'Being an architect, I'm attracted to the physical form,' Mark explains. 'The gems are very architectural in the way they evolve with the octagonal and hexagonal shapes. The colours are for the most part earth tones, although we do have some gems that are more colourful, such as the amethyst and malachite. There is a variety.'

Eloise adds: 'It actually got started for me when I was a young teenager.' She began collecting stones while growing up in Palm Springs, California. 'My first stone was a little piece of sandstone with lots of circular plates. I found it at a gem show off the side of the road, and I thought it was fascinating. We have since collected much more substantial and interesting types of rocks, but that was my beginning rock, which I still have.'

The couple's collection comprises predominantly monumental objects that fit like pieces of furniture into their house, which they can admire from afar, rather than jewel-like miniatures that need to be displayed in a case and examined close up. 'As we became a bit more secure financially, we could afford to splurge on the bigger, rarer crystals that feel all the more special,' Mark says.

From a whopper of an ammonite to an earth-toned felanite, whose blades in various sizes and shapes are formed upside down in the dried-up riverbeds of the desert, the common thread running through the collection is the sculptural quality of the pieces, as well as the provenance of how they came about. This is what guides them. 'Knowing the history and the background of a piece is a huge attraction for me,' Eloise notes. 'I have a piece of wood from a Polish salt mine that was a ladder, sunk into the waters. Salt crystals grew on the timber frame and when they closed the mine, they cut it up and sold the pieces. When I look at that, the crystals are so interesting with their sharp edges, but also the fact of knowing how it grew is of interest to me.'

She continues: 'The agatized coral is also a wonderful piece. This is coral that came out of the water beds in Florida, which over time has fossilized. They look like big chunks of rock, but when you slice them open, you see these beautiful whites and blues, as well as different shapes formed by the coral. It's fascinating to know where something came from and how it got formed.'

The couple buy mostly from the Tucson Gem and Mineral Show in Arizona, an international forum for serious rock collecting that brings together dealers from all over the world in one location. 'It's kind of like a treasure hunt,' says Mark. 'It's exciting.'

Eloise agrees. 'These are definitely treasures. They are exciting in their beauty. Bringing a rock home gives us the memories of looking for it and also an appreciation for all the different parts of the world where these incredible pieces are created.' Reflecting on her lifelong captivation for crystals and rocks, she adds: 'What I would really love to do is go to Wyoming, to the Green River Valley and search for fossils myself. I think to myself, in this life I did educational evaluation. My goal in my next life is to somehow or other be a geologist. I would like to spend more time actually in the field, finding these things, as opposed to going to Tucson.'

'IT'S KIND OF LIKE A TREASURE HUNT.
IT'S EXCITING.'

Upstairs in the kitchen and living room, the palette has plenty of warmth from the earthy sandstones and fossils on display. Most of the rocks were bought by the couple at the Tucson Gem and Mineral Show and are displayed simply on Lucite stands.

MARK AND ELOISE APPEL

Mark's treasured collection of malachite is displayed in the bedroom, where the uniformity of the green stands out against the white walls and shelving. The amorphous, varied stones are also reputed to have spiritual and healing properties. 'When people are sick, healers will bring pieces of malachite in to help with the recovery process,' says Eloise.

MARK AND
ELOISE'S TIPS
FOR BUYING AT
MINERALS AND
GEMS FAIRS

1 Be prepared. It's a good idea to obtain any exhibition catalogues in advance of the fair opening.

2 Allow time for asking questions. The settings are intimate, so you can get to know the exhibitors and their products.

3 Negotiate and compare prices between vendors. The price is always to do with the quality, but some vendors will sell at keystone, which is half the listed price.

4 Spend the first day looking, the second day buying and the third day enjoying the incredible pieces you could never afford. It is comparable to going to a natural-history museum and getting to stand right next to a dinosaur.

5 The end of a show is a good time to negotiate. The dealers won't want to cart any really heavy items home. Buy with placement in mind, but whatever catches your fancy.

MARK AND ELOISE APPEL

'IT'S FASCINATING TO KNOW WHERE SOMETHING
CAME FROM AND HOW IT GOT FORMED.'

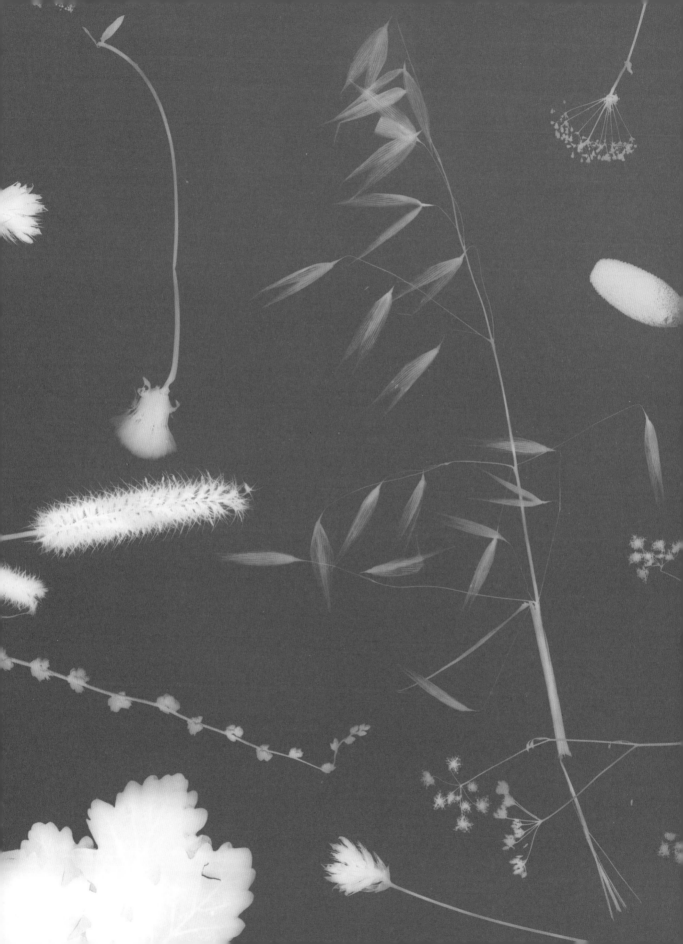

INTO THE WOODS

FINDING FORM
Spencer Fung, London, UK

Describing himself as an accidental botanist, architect and artist, Spencer Fung has a habit of collecting items that include spiky tree husks, fossilized rocks and interesting pieces of bark. He is drawn to life's little details and spots nature's gifts wherever he goes, whether gathering a collection of fallen alder leaves from nearby Hampstead Heath, chosen for the subtle brown colour that he finds divine, or making a collage of leaf compositions in his sketchbook to serve as a record of nature, as well as inspiration for his work. Seeds are a constant. 'I love collecting seeds, I find them irresistible,' he says. 'They are like little works of art, sculpted by nature.' Spencer's work is extremely responsive to his surroundings, and the strands of this love for the natural world are evident in his home.

In this renovated Victorian house, period features have been retained, and antique grey marble used to define the ground floor. Spencer designed much of the furniture, including the white oak dining table and twin glass-fronted display cabinets that house his large collection of china.

In the cabinet in the study, objects are not styled but are an accumulation, layer upon layer. 'One much-loved item is a magnolia seed head from Catalonia, which Spencer picked up before we had children,' says his wife Teresa. 'We don't need a photograph album. These are our memories.'

Throughout the house, sea urchins, pine cones and fossils are displayed together – sometimes casually, sometimes in a more considered fashion. The collection speaks of family history, as well as telling a story through their beautiful textures and shapes.

Spencer Fung is known for his meticulously crafted architecture and furniture designs, which weave together manmade and natural materials. Much of his inspiration stems from a reverence for the natural world, evidenced in the bits and bobs that are dotted about his London home. Here, you will find lumps of rock salt brought back as souvenirs from a salt mine Spencer and his creative-director wife Teresa Roviras visited in her native Catalonia, a pebble ensemble inspired by a trip to Kettle's Yard in Cambridge, and countless pieces of coral that washed up on the beach in Hong Kong after a storm.

'The message from this is so clear,' Spencer says of the flotsam coral. 'We can see how fragile our environment is. We need to commit to repairing decades of wrongdoing. Nature is endangered. We have reached the point where future generations may be deprived of the natural heritage we take for granted. In California, for instance, the Sequoias may look majestic from the ground, but the tops of these 4,000-year-old giants are suffering from disease that threatens their existence. Everywhere I go, I see a precarious situation. We need to take action urgently'.

Spencer and Teresa both grew up connected to the natural world, but from different backgrounds. Teresa is from a rich Latin culture, whereas Spencer describes his perspective as more tranquil. 'Teresa's family live in Catalonia, close to a natural park, so walks and hikes are part of our routine during the holidays,' he says. 'Nature is our common love. I'm not a deliberate collector, but I will always have a pebble in my palm, or something I picked up and put in my pocket.'

In the house, nature is everywhere, from the wide borders of grey-veined marble framing the reception rooms to the smooth, bone-coloured lime plaster that imparts a sense of comfort to the walls. The interior is ingrained with layers of natural texture and a palette that connects with the outside. Decorative schemes don't get more tactile than this, and the natural palette also serves as a spectacular backdrop for displaying furniture, works of art and other objects.

It is this presentation that is key to how Spencer's collection shapes the dynamic of his home. He will take something humble and ordinary – a pebble or a shell – and place it carefully, treating it as if it were made from gold. Often, items are left in isolation, such as the hero piece of old driftwood in the hall. Mounted on its own, it is elevated to a work of art. Elsewhere items are grouped, like the combination of pewter, Jurassic rock and cracked fossils on the kitchen shelves. One informs the other. You can mix and match the dark with the beige; they all work with each other and never clash.

'That's the joy of working with nature,' Spencer explains. 'These things aren't particularly rare, nor are they expensive. They are common objects that are often overlooked. But when I see these items, I see a thread – whether it's the texture, patina or shape – that becomes artistic and evokes a Henry Moore sketch or a Ben Nicholson relief. Our home is testament to the beauty of nature'.

Items like the antlers on the coffee table and sea urchin on the shelf are placed in isolation for their sculptural beauty. *Overleaf* In the bedroom, the circle of pebbles is Teresa's ode to Kettle's Yard in Cambridge. 'There is something very pleasing about the weight and shape of the pebbles when you hold them in your hand,' she says.

'I FIND SEEDS IRRESISTIBLE. THEY ARE LIKE LITTLE
WORKS OF ART, SCULPTED BY NATURE.'

'THAT'S THE JOY OF WORKING WITH NATURE.
WHEN I SEE THESE ITEMS, I SEE A THREAD – WHETHER
IT'S THE TEXTURE, PATINA OR SHAPE.'

Spencer creates artworks using earth pigments, charcoal and graphite, which pick up on the details he finds in the everyday. 'Nature has such beautiful textures,' he says. 'The seeds, coral and stone share similar patterns and curves. I love sketching them. It's so satisfying.'

SPENCER'S
TIPS FOR
USING NATURE
TO INSPIRE A
DECORATIVE
SCHEME

1 Try using natural materials wherever possible. The textures and patina cannot be replicated with manmade alternatives.

2 Look to nature to decide on a colour palette. If it works in nature, it is also likely to work in your home.

3 Some of the best decorations are from nature. You don't have to buy new things. Instead, use found items for the natural beauty of their design.

4 A good way to observe nature up close is to germinate seeds in an avocado glass, as you get to nurture and watch your plant grow. It's a slow growth, but you realize there is as much life in the roots below. Nature is so much bigger than us in many ways.

'I'M NOT A DELIBERATE COLLECTOR, BUT I ALWAYS
HAVE A PEBBLE IN MY PALM, OR SOMETHING I PICKED
UP AND PUT MY POCKET.'

INSPIRED BY BLOOMSBURY
Shhh My Darling, Gildone, Italy

At this three-storey house in the Apennine mountains in southern Italy, artist and makers Jenny Schenal and Graziano Farinaccio have made their mark with eclectic collections of antique finds and their own decorative touches. Influenced by the murals and painted furniture at Charleston in East Sussex, the home of artists Vanessa Bell and Duncan Grant, the result is decorative and colourful. And for this husband-and-wife duo, collecting is a way of life. As illustrators of bespoke wedding invitations, it is the decorative aspect of items such as antlers, feathers and butterflies that interests them most. Everything is recorded by drawing it. Like Bell and Grant at Charleston, their passion for collecting is connected to a deep interest in art.

In the living room, a 1970s taxidermy deer from a private seller in Paris adds sweetness to the large fireplace, which throws heat into this hilltop house during the winter. It is framed in a glass box, giving a museum-like feel; a found branch looks striking against the all-white walls.

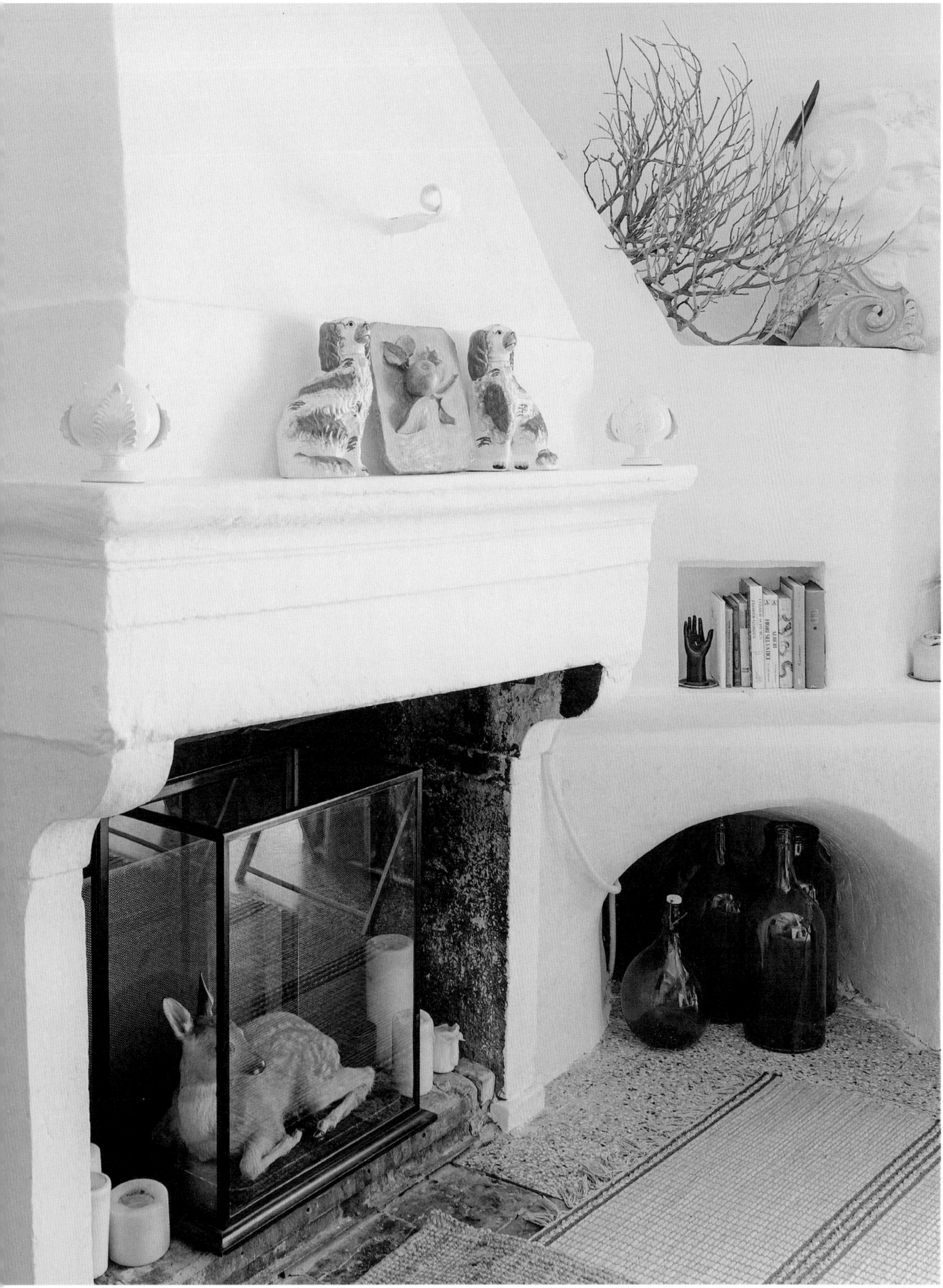

Dried flower heads, skulls and butterflies have been used to decorate this terraced home in the pretty hill town of Gildone in southern Italy, high up in the Apennine mountains.

The wreath was made using leaves from an oak, one of the most popular trees in the region. 'This room was hard to decorate because of the large fireplace,' Jenny says. 'We wanted to put something in that wasn't too heavy, but decorative at the same time.'

An artist's home is many things. It is a source of creativity, a treasure chest full of surprises, a place where personal aesthetics are expressed freely, often through the objects kept inside. Jenny and Graziano have always been avid collectors, beginning with costume jewelry, old toys and vintage illustrated children's books. But since moving from their apartment in Rome to Gra's grandmother's home in the country, gathering items from the natural world became all the more relevant.

'We work from home, and all of these natural elements help to create a relaxing environment,' Jenny explains. 'We have kept the soul of the house – everything is exactly as it was – but have added our own collections. These are all things found in the woods that caught our eye.'

Displayed as altar-like installations, cluttered on top of vintage furniture sourced from flea markets or family hand-me-downs, objects include a horse's pelvic bone filled with dried posies, a vase of artichokes, a wreath made from oak twigs, and more. In keeping with the Bloomsbury aesthetic, Renaissance influences and paisley patterns feature throughout the interior and humble objects have been transformed with paint and imagination. In the bedroom, Gra decorated a chest of drawers from Ikea with Grecian motifs, and the wall of the study now features an exotic fresco, inspired by the handpainted wallpapers of de Gournay. 'This room is the place where we work, so we wanted it to be inspiring,' Jenny says. 'It's important to have a nice view.'

As artists, the couple have a good instinct for creating visual impact. They play with scale, varying the sizes of their dried flower arrangements to emphasize each item. In the living room, the large oak-branch wreath is a focal point and balances the scale of the fireplace. Jenny and Gra also like to source unique pieces and admit to being Francophiles when it comes to flea-market shopping, with Porte de Clignancourt in Paris a favourite destination for finding art. It's these accessories, including the reproduction of a portrait by the Netherlandish artist Petrus Christus in the bedroom with a framed butterfly above, which add personality to a space. 'It's things with a decorative aspect that hold the most fascination for us,' Jenny says. 'We're illustrators. We look at something with a view to painting it.'

The legacy of the artist as naturalist goes back centuries, gaining momentum at the end of the 15th century and carrying through to the 19th century, when important botanical and maritime discoveries brought scientific study of the natural world to the fore, as well as satisfying a taste for exoticism. The natural-history painter travelled extensively, and would return from far-flung expeditions to recreate the grandeur of nature by either drawing from preserved samples or cultivating plant specimens at home.

A zoological and floral theme influences Jenny and Gra's illustrations, and their designs bring purpose to their collections, as seen in their studio with the picturesque Byzantine wall. Despite their extensive collections of vintage furniture and natural objects, the effect of the interior scheme is curated, not cluttered. The look is light as air, with lots of white space around pieces and groups are kept together in dense patches. 'We try not to be led by too much stuff,' says Jenny, who is keen to hit the right note between being surrounded by items she is inspired by, while keeping the ambience clean. 'That said, we're definitely not minimal.'

The Bloomsbury artists embraced all things creative through a love of textiles, eclectic collections and painted surfaces. In this romantic bedroom, a pair of antlers support a canopy of pink-striped curtains, which in turn frame a favourite painting and an artwork of a butterfly.

'WE'RE ILLUSTRATORS. WE LOOK AT SOMETHING
WITH A VIEW TO PAINTING IT.'

'IT'S THINGS WITH A DECORATIVE ASPECT
THAT HOLD THE MOST FASCINATION FOR US.'

The chest of drawers is from Ikea, painted by Gra in a decorative scheme inspired by Bloomsbury. 'This is the mix we like,' Gra says. 'Natural references and Greek art in a rural setting.'

In the study, a stuffed heron from the 1930s suits the palm-tree mural painted by Gra, inspired by an existing Liberty stencil running across the top of the space. The bird was bought in Paris during a trip to the taxidermy specialists Deyrolle, where the couple's fixation with natural history began.

JENNY AND GRA'S HINTS FOR DISPLAYING NATURE IN THE HOME

1 To add vitality to a space, don't be afraid to paint surfaces, including walls and furniture (tables, chairs, bookcases). We take themes from the Italian Renaissance as our cue, using vivid colours that stand out. Artists such as Henri Matisse and the Fauves are a good starting point for inspiration.

2 To add personality and create a focal point in a room, choose voluminous flower displays over small ones. We are not botanists or flower designers, but we like to use flowers and greenery to decorate our house.

3 For flowers that last a long time, look for plants that are sturdy when dried. Artichoke flowers, wild chicory, ferns, hydrangeas and thistles are all good for this.

4 To make a striking impression, we prefer single-variety flower arrangements, as they are simpler and easy to find in nature.

5 If you have a large empty wall, go bold with a wide wreath instead of a small one. For the base, use long, light branches (such as willow) that bend easily and shape into a circle, using twine, raffia or thin wire to hold in place. Add dried foliage, either round the entire body or just part of it.

6 For an alternative to flowers, gather a bunch of feathers and display in a vase. Long, narrow feathers, like those from peacock tails, can be arranged into old-fashioned fans.

7 Group objects by colour or type, which helps a collection look more cohesive. Alternate hyper-decorated spaces with emptier ones for balance.

'WE WORK FROM HOME, AND ALL OF THESE NATURAL ELEMENTS HELP TO CREATE A RELAXING ENVIRONMENT.'

A COSMOS OF EARTH'S RAW MATERIALS
Michele Oka Doner, New York, USA

An archival bench sculpted from Cuban mahogany, large-scale minerals, bark from a fallen baobab tree, embedded fossils displayed on a marble tabletop and glass platters holding an assortment of seeds – this Manhattan loft apartment is crammed with treasures from the natural world, whether used by artist/homeowner Michele Oka Doner for making sculptures or for simply living with. Through the tall windows overlooking the inner-city streets of SoHo, nature and all of its incredible ancestry creeps into this modern-day cave.

Michele holds a fragment of bark from a baobab tree in Kenya, now a permanent feature of the studio. 'A friend and I went on a pilgrimage to visit the oldest baobab tree, setting off early and driving for miles,' she says. 'When we arrived, a local told us the tree had collapsed three weeks earlier. We continued anyway, and I retrieved this piece. The wood has enormous energy and great tension – only Mother Nature is capable of such a feat.'

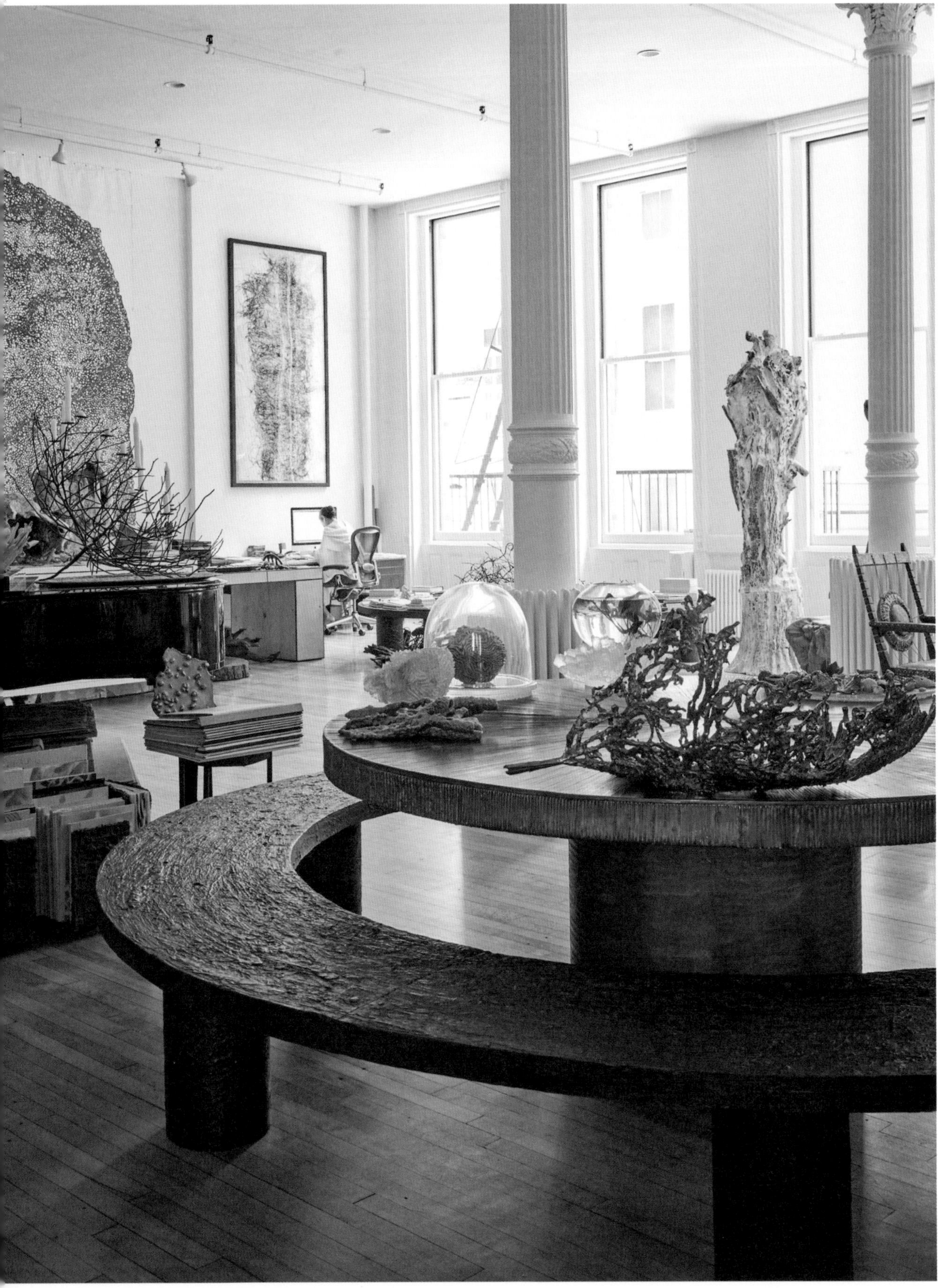

Michele describes her studio/home as an Italian piazza, differentiated by use, not walls. Everything is fluid and can be pushed aside, so the whole floor can be used to lay out a project. Throughout the apartment, seeds, dried leaves and ancient stones are displayed alongside works such as her circular bronze 'Ice Ring' bench and bronze 'Radiant' table.

Found objects are stored in a drawer unit on casters. On the far wall is an enormous drawing of mother-of-pearl under a microscope. The lines illustrate how a mollusc secretes nacre in irregular patterns, causing the surface to catch the light and create the opalescence associated with pearls. Only half of the drawing is seen; the rest remains rolled up and hidden away.

Michele Oka Doner insists she is not a collector, yet the walls, floor and tabletops of her New York loft apartment are teeming with rocks, leaves and bones. It betrays a fascination with the world of natural history with which she clearly likes to surround herself. 'The intention isn't a deliberate act to accumulate,' she says. 'It's just that over the years I have picked up a stone that was particularly beautiful, or a piece of wood that has a crack forming a beautiful line.'

By bringing home these organic materials to study, Michele has embedded her live/work space with ancestral fragments and forms she has been seduced by when out walking, been given or bought herself. In one spot there is a bone from a tree, in another, there's a dried leaf from the ginkgo plant in the corner. 'This is not a collection in my mind,' she explains. 'This is about living in a natural way with natural forms. It's part of my life.'

Michele's interest in geology stems from a childhood growing up in Miami Beach, and particularly from a favourite banyan tree close to her house: 'We have a connection to nature that predates language. This tree has been my companion through a lifetime.' She also recalls a booklet she produced at the age of twelve or thirteen on the International Geophysical Year, a response to the Sputnik launch in 1957: 'Everybody was very excited, but also fearful. It was the Cold War, and there was that feeling that Russia could see us. I remember standing outside my house and looking up at the sky.'

She has always made associations between shapes, between coral branches found on the beach and the veins in her hand or a leaf. 'Things call out to me that have texture and shape,' she says. 'I find out later that it could be a piece of a meteor or a shard of volcanic glass brought back from somewhere. These fragments are mysterious. I'm only finding part of a story.' For Michele, these pieces are shorthand for life processes we don't really see the whole of. 'We can only grasp the storm,' she adds. 'We don't see it forming.'

This glimpse into the cosmos and enchantment with the formation of the earth speak to Michele of mystery and magic, which is part of what she has created here. When she moved into this Italianate-style brownstone, a former button factory, in 1981, the light flowing in from the long windows and the majesty of the open-plan space were the main draws. Like a contemporary cave, the vast interior is differentiated by use, not by walls. 'It's very fluid,' she says. 'It's actually very right-brain, in that you can flow and move around. It's not a grid.'

Upon entering the apartment, you are faced with a collection of porcelain soul-catcher totems, positioned in places of ceremony or significance. Here, they are mounted on the curved metal wall as a form of protection. The space is furnished minimally, with works of art, rocks and fossils providing texture, colour and structure, rather than decoration. There is no separation between home life and work – just as it was originally intended in its button-factory days.

'I have exactly what I am able to live with,' says Michele. 'I'm living with the conveniences of modern medicine and science. I have electricity and warmth, and yet I'm able to behave like an ancient woman. I walk to the farmers' market. I bring back raw materials. I grind, I cook. It's very lovely to compress many centuries of the world into my life living here.'

Hanging near the entrance is a group of glazed porcelain 'soul-catchers', which have the appearance of being eroded away by ocean currents. The assemblages of wood, roots and other materials are used in making sculptures, and are part of a lifetime spent observing the natural world.

'THIS IS NOT A COLLECTION IN MY MIND. THIS IS ABOUT LIVING IN A NATURAL WAY WITH NATURAL FORMS. IT'S PART OF MY LIFE.'

'THINGS CALL OUT TO ME THAT HAVE
TEXTURE AND SHAPE.'

In the breakfast room, two large figurative works by Michele are propped up against the wall. She also designed the dining table, which is topped in dark grey marble. In the hallway, the marble top of the console contains a multitude of embedded fossils.

Forming an altar of sorts, Michele's 'Radiant Disk' presentation platter contains a collection of seeds – an assortment that changes with the season – along with finds discovered in the neighbourhood or in the woods around New York, or from visits to Miami Beach.

MICHELE'S
GUIDE TO USING
ANCIENT IDEAS
FOR OBJECT
ARRANGEMENT

1 Think about positioning favourite items in places of ceremony or significance. I like to place my soul-catchers at the
entrance as amulets.

2 For a less visually distracting view, try borrowing the
Japanese idea of positioning items where the eye would go,
at waist height or lower. When the main view is low, the
space feels quiet.

3 Keep items on rotation so that they remain fresh. These
could be avocados ripening in the kitchen, or a rosebud
in a tiny glass – even a leaf will do. I pick up fallen golden
ginkgo leaves in the autumn. Choose the best one, and lay
it on a table as if it was actually gold.

4 Always keep things seasonal. I bring home produce from
the local farmers' market, which reminds me that it is
springtime or late autumn.

5 Herbs are another constant. Mint can be kept in a vase for
flowers. The aroma is wonderful, and the leaves find their
way into tea and sauces.

6 Look at the shapes and materials of objects and group these
together. When I find stones or fragments of shell or glass,
I like to put them in similar categories for companionship.

'WE HAVE A CONNECTION TO NATURE
THAT PREDATES LANGUAGE.'

THE BEAUTY OF FOREST FINDS
Christina Ahlefeldt-Laurvig, Rensow, Germany

For some people, nature is at the very heart of what they do. At this old manor house in a village two hours north of Berlin, the foraged installations betray the homeowner's fascination with natural history. There is a Narnia-like woodland scheme – gnarled branches reach up to the ceiling, bunches of preserved grapes hang from vintage chandeliers and feathers appear everywhere, earmarking books and adding plumage to pictures on the wall. The shared vision of Danish-born Christina Ahlefeldt-Laurvig and her husband Knut Splett-Henning for their home and guest house takes a walk on the wild, wooded side, filling them with creations and works of art made out of simple items from nature.

Filled with antiques and handcrafted objects, this baroque house in rural Mecklenburg is surrounded by a wild park of centuries-old trees, deer and peacocks.

Many of the foraged items have been repurposed and used in unexpected ways, with hollowed-out trees serving as bowls and dried bunches of grapes and vine leaves hanging from the chandelier. 'The grapes looked so pretty, I thought it was a shame to eat them,' says Christina.

CHRISTINA AHLEFELDT-LAURVIG

'We find beauty in things where other people don't necessarily place value,' says Christina Ahlefeldt-Laurvig of the forest-found collections on display in her home. These include a huge piece of bark from a willow tree, chosen for its intricate structure, or storm-fallen mistletoe, discovered while driving through the rural Mecklenburg countryside. For Christina, the value lies in the discovery of these natural gifts, as there is a huge amount of coincidence at play; the tricky part is getting them home. 'That's why I have a crooked back,' laughs Knut, who is used to filling the van up with fallen pieces of wood and hunks of stone.

Christina's mother was an Ikebana teacher, so she grew up surrounded by the creative women who practised the Japanese art of flower arranging. From them, she learned the language of proportion and form. 'For me, the branch is the arrangement,' she explains of her sculptural compositions, which, whether oversized or miniature, are simple at heart. Like an alchemist, she can transform a humble branch into an item of worth.

Her career trajectory spans fashion, interior design and styling, as well as set design for films, but her obsession with collecting started young. 'Growing up at the seaside near Copenhagen, I was always looking for special shells and driftwood,' she remembers. 'I've always been looking. My mother will tell you that even as a child my pockets were always full. It's like being a shopaholic – I have to take these things home.'

Christina has drawers full of remnants she has picked up from each trip to the forest. Like Little Red Riding Hood, her basket comes home filled to the brim. 'When other people find interesting items in the woods, they bring them to me,' she says. This includes her children, who are pros at spotting bugs at low level. They find many things, from bumblebees to leaves and acorns, which Christina uses to create jewelry or compositions under glass domes. 'It's a joy for them,' she says. Away from the tradition of curiosity cabinets, there isn't a scientific approach to her collecting: 'It's all for the love of nature. I would never kill an animal. All the items I've collected have passed away naturally and fallen in the woods.'

Living between different eras in their countryside bubble, Christina and Knut find that the interactions between nature, art and their home are constant. Furniture is moved around as newly found branches are brought in. 'Things are never static,' Knut says of the decoration. It's part of the appeal for the guests who come to stay. Among the house's charms are enormous branches that meander every which way. Collected logs and boughs jostle for space with delicate bird's nests, giant pine cones and forest mushrooms. The walls are painted purple and hung with vintage textiles. Romantic and rugged, there is so much natural history in this timber-framed building, from the materials it was originally built with to the foraged, eclectic decor.

'The entire house was built with nature around it,' Knut adds, referring to the energy of the 17th-century construction. 'The foundation is built on granite and all the walls are clay. The bricks were baked on site and the timber structure is from the woodland nearby. If the house were to fall down, everything would go back to the earth.'

Leather-bound volumes are bookmarked with various owl feathers found in barns and attics, and an oak figurine is decorated with peacock feathers discovered on walks through the woods.

'WE FIND BEAUTY IN THINGS WHERE OTHER PEOPLE
DON'T NECESSARILY PLACE VALUE.'

To create a sense of order to items displayed on the walls, Christina has used antique rugs and empty picture frames to contain her collections. The textiles provide an interesting backdrop and the frames themselves become part of the decoration.

Christina doesn't overdo her displays, and keeps it natural. 'I leave pieces as I found them,' she says. 'It's about keeping to the natural form, and finding the right spot in the house to place them.' In the bedroom, antlers are draped with dried fennel, poppy pods, thistles and peacock feathers – all displayed against a wall-mounted antique rug.

1 For a dramatic wall display, combine objects from nature against a textile wall hanging. An empty vintage frame also works well. Allow for one branch to be larger – pieces look better if they appear as if they are about to escape.

2 To make an eye-catching table centrepiece, think about symmetry as a starting point and gather items with varying textures and heights around it. Two candlesticks placed off-centre on a table look wonderful with foraged items. You can use a branch for hanging items to create even more interest.

3 Stick to a single colour scheme. This will make all the different materials work together as one.

4 For a unique chandelier, experiment with dried flowers, leaves and fruit. You can use these as ornaments, and change them according to time of year.

5 Don't feel as though any change to a room's decoration or arrangement is permanent. Everything is temporary, and you can add or remove elements over time. Like the natural objects, the process is organic, too.

6 You can always find wonderful sculptures in nature. Remember to keep your eyes open.

CHRISTINA AHLEFELDT-LAURVIG

'MY MOTHER WILL TELL YOU THAT EVEN AS A CHILD MY POCKETS WERE ALWAYS FULL. IT'S LIKE BEING A SHOPAHOLIC – I HAVE TO TAKE THESE THINGS HOME.'

HOUSE OF HORTICULTURE

A NATURALIST'S WILDLY COLOURFUL HOME
Marian McEvoy, Upstate New York, USA

Looking to brighten a room? Try adding feathers to a lamp-shade. Or better still, why not add pine cones in a geometrical pattern to the ceiling? These are just two ideas going on in this homespun interior, where the artisan-owner uses her collections of pressed flowers, acorns and leaves to add flair. In the 18th century, shellwork and collage were popular handicrafts among 'educated women', reflecting a taste for all things decorative and a growing fascination with the curiosities of the natural world. The same notion is at play here, where a dedication to experimentation and working with nature has created an utterly joyful home.

Artist and former interiors editor Marian McEvoy uses plants as inspiration for her home decor. She tames the wilderness by framing organic shapes with borders, and veers towards symmetry wherever she can.

Marian leaves plenty of background space in her collages to give a fresh, clean and modern look to the finished piece. The same principle is used in her approach to interior decoration, with off-white walls setting off the botanicals beautifully.

In the living room, the combination of coral, red and cream makes each colour look spectacular. 'I tend to love the colours on the warmer end of the scale,' Marian explains. 'Using shades from the same section of the colour wheel gives a feeling of order and harmony.'

The word 'collector' sounds so serious. It conjures up images of curators and librarians, classification and the study of forms. More light-heartedly, it's a hobby, and for this chicest of hunter gatherers, collecting is about inspiring interior design.

Deep in Upstate New York, snuggled in the Hudson Valley and surrounded by lots of animals and trees, this is home to Marian McEvoy, botanical artist, painter, designer, decorator, founding editor of *Elle Decor* and super-craft queen. She is a bon vivant when it comes to nature and design, and her cottage-industry home is testament to her love of embellishing interiors with natural finds. Savvy with her decorating energy, she has made feature walls and ceilings out of pine cones and ribbons, created parrot-like mirrors done up with exotic feathers, and marks up paper lampshades with pens to make them stand out. For Marian, it's not about collecting for collecting's sake. It's what you do with the results of your forays that counts.

'Celebrating the gifts of nature is a starting point for me,' she says about her desire to bring fallen leaves and seeds home for experimenting with in artworks and decoration. 'I'm constantly finding things that happen to go very well with some of my French furniture and my American stuff, too. To me, there's absolutely no problem combining something primitive and natural with something perhaps more sophisticated. As a matter of fact, they complement each other. I think too much manmade makes a house looks look like a showroom, and too much nature makes it look like a summer camp. I don't want either of those. I'd like a little of both.'

There are perhaps thousands of objects from the natural world in Marian's home. Most items are found, either by chance while on a walk or going out into her back garden. 'Dead trees are one of my favourite things,' she says. 'Not the tree itself, but the fungi that grows on them. I would decorate a whole wall with them if I could find enough.'

Raised in California, it was these early years spent on the West Coast where her fascination with collecting and pattern-making began. Order is key to Marian's psyche, which you can see not only in her collages, but also in her rooms. Nearly every piece of furniture, wall or window is framed in some way. 'Borders mean order to me,' she notes. 'Yes, you can have a mad display of tree fungi on a table, but isn't it nice that the sofa alongside looks tailored and crisp in a manicured way? Somehow, there has to be an element of logic. I don't collect a big box of pine cones and then throw them on a low table or shelf. I like to arrange and corral.'

Marian's Hudson River home connects the inside with the outside, showcasing both the organic and polished sides of her decorating taste. Most of the colour is not a natural situation. The neutrals come from the pine cones, acorns, fungi, bird's and wasp's nests and old pieces of wood that she loves, and sometimes she will paint them. 'I'm not a purist, let's put it like that,' she admits.

The finished look is far from a crazy, turn-of-the-century antiques shop. It is ruthlessly edited, especially at the change of the seasons. 'When the temperatures go down, you use your house in different ways,' she explains. 'I may look at my Winter Room, thinking that bird's-nest collection doesn't look robust or warm enough. I might add a few more. Or I might get rid of some of that coral. It just looks shabby. I'm the same way with my wardrobe. I'll just go in the closet and say, I don't wear this thing – bang, boom.'

This is what she is all about, and what we all need a jolt of right now – more personality, soul-lifting colours and updated homeware that deliver instant cheer. Find nature. Go play.

The all-white mirror in the master bedroom was created by shell artist Tess Morley. 'It is so impeccably perfect,' Marian says. 'I look at it and think, why can't my headboard look more like that?' Same-size collages using similar elements look great in groups of two, three or ten. The challenge is to create designs that are siblings, but are not identical.

MARIAN McEVOY

'CELEBRATING THE GIFTS OF NATURE
IS A STARTING POINT FOR ME.'

In the craft room, Marian's extensive collection is contained in baskets, with the skirted work bench hiding any mess. She creates her graphic, geometric patterns by combining various types and sizes of leaves, and adds movement and dimension by using slightly curved stems, rather than straight sticks, which can look stiff and flat.

1 Think shape first, and colour second. If you like the size and contour of a leaf, bud or flower, pick it with a bit of stem attached, and press it within a couple hours of cutting.

2 Be aware that the colours of a live plant will alter during the pressing process. Bright greens will not stay bright green. Colours might deepen and appear more muddied.

3 The thinner the leaf, stem or flower, the easier it will be to press.

4 To soak up moisture, try using blotting paper or newsprint, replacing the sheets every few days. I do not use a professional flower press, but rather wooden boards, sheets of plain newsprint and stacks of large books piled on top.

5 Once dry and flattened, leaves and flowers can be stored, layered carefully, in shallow, uncovered wicker, cardboard or wooden boxes. Keep them away from direct sunlight.

6 As for gluing, start with a base of good-quality thick paper. I use hefty matting board for large pieces and sturdy watercolour paper for smaller collages.

7 The type of glue needed depends on the thickness and suppleness of the plant. For a large hollyhock, spray adhesive works well. Flatten in place for fifteen minutes with heavy books or a box of rocks.

8 To glue very thin petals or leaves, use tweezers to put them in place on the paper. I then gently lift the edges and apply a diluted liquid matt glue with a tiny, natural-bristled paintbrush. You need patience and steady hands.

9 A final must: as all botanicals are extremely fragile and will fade over time, frame them tightly under glass or treated Plexiglas, away from sunlight.

'I DON'T COLLECT A BIG BOX OF PINE CONES
AND THEN THROW THEM ON A LOW TABLE OR SHELF.
I LIKE TO ARRANGE AND CORRAL.'

MARIAN MCEVOY

THE ALLURE OF ORCHIDS
Sean Barton, Macclesfield, UK

There is a certain level of decadence associated with the Victorian era, and when it comes to the Victorians' love for preserving plants and introducing nature into the home, this home is no exception. This is when the frenzy for orchid hunting began, with wealthy patrons dispatching intrepid naturalists to South America and the South Pacific to search out the most elusive plants. It is also when the fashion for creating elegant micro-worlds under glass took off. Indoor gardens and glass terrariums decorate every corner of this botanist-collector's home, while macabre portraits, velvet scroll-arm sofas and ornate chandeliers create moments worthy of any Brontë novel. In modern-day rural England, orchidelirium lives on.

Along with his jewel-like orchids, Sean Barton is also a fan of large-scale plants. The *Brassaiopsis dumicola* in the living room was chosen to add drama and make the most of the ceiling height. The plant is a recent introduction to the UK from Vietnam by plant hunters Sue and Bleddyn Wynn-Jones. In contrast, the little *Lepanthes regularis* orchid underneath a glass dome becomes a beautiful object of love.

In many ways, Sean's enthusiasm for British horticulture harks back to the 19th-century obsession with collecting plants, including ferns. Terrariums are a great way to bring greenery indoors, either as open micro-worlds or housed under glass, depending on which plants are used.

In the dining room, the cabinets and tabletops teem with taxidermy, antique prints of flora and fauna, vintage chandelier crystals and favourite plants. The curated display demonstrates Sean's love for natural history, which he explores each day in his work as a florist, gardener and orchid specialist.

You know that feeling when you move into a new house and all of your furniture suddenly fits? This was how it was for plantsman Sean Barton when he moved from a basic 1990s semi to this handsome Victorian property in Macclesfield, Cheshire, a silk-weaving town in the northwest of England. It's a stretch to imagine his Wunderkammer collection of eye-catching plants and antique finds on display within a modern house, but when he relocated to this 19th-century gatehouse, everything clicked.

Each room, and almost every surface, is tricked out with items from the world of natural history. From the coffee table in the living room, crammed with an assortment of candelabra and rare taxidermy, to the fern-filled entrance with its magnificent antler chandelier, Victorian-inspired botany is combined with a respect for nature and a fascination with collecting eccentric treasures.

'As a child, I was always into plants, snakes and bugs,' Sean explains. 'I remember going on holiday and finding a rabbit's skull under a hedge, which I wasn't allowed to bring home. I thought it was amazing.' His parents would buy him taxidermy for Christmas, rather than *Star Wars* figures, and this evolved into collecting rarer and more exotic finds.

A former head gardener at Henbury Hall in Cheshire, Sean's interest in orchids was unleashed when he first saw one as a child at a garden centre and thought it was the best thing ever. 'At the time, it was an unusual choice,' he explains. 'A hybrid *Vuylstekeara* Cambria "Plush" that you just can't find anymore.'

This perhaps accounts for how his obsession with orchids began. 'I'm possessed by them really,' he concedes. 'I like how diverse they are. When you say "orchids" to people, they think of the ones in Marks & Spencer, but there are about 30,000 species. I don't think of them as plants, really. They're like pets. There are so many thousands of them, it's endlessly fascinating.'

Sean is a judge for the Orchid Society of Great Britain and is always on the lookout for the next orchid, which he buys direct from Ecuadorian dealers who visit the UK a couple of times a year. He goes for cool climate orchids from the cloud-forests of the Andes – the more peculiar and unusually shaped, the better – all meticulously tended in a converted outbuilding in the garden. One example may feature leaves covered in thousands of tiny purple hairs giving an intense colour and a soft, velvety texture, another might be so tiny it resembles a precious jewel. Yet another might look almost vampiric, such as the *Dracula chimaera* on display under the large glass cylinder in the dining room.

A fan of all things Dickensian, this carries through to his taste in interior decoration. Sean prefers wintry colours and candlelit rooms, adding plants and flowers against the dark backdrops. 'I love museums,' he says of the mood he creates in his home. 'I also used to love going into bookshops and sniffing the books, which probably sounds a bit strange. To some this may seem gothic, but to me, gothic means purple curtains.' He is, however, happy cultivating spider's webs.

'WHEN YOU SAY "ORCHIDS" TO PEOPLE, THEY THINK OF THE ONES IN MARKS & SPENCER, BUT THERE ARE ABOUT 30,000 SPECIES.'

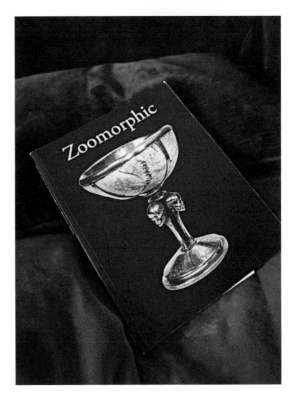

A shift away from the fussiness of collecting, Sean favours a less ordered arrangement. Here, a mature coco de mer sea coconut is positioned on the seat of an old chair with a portrait propped up behind – mainly to stop people sitting on it.

The sombre palette of the entrance, along with the antler chandelier, sawfish skeleton and giant clam assemblage, gives a museum-like quality to the space that Sean loves. The ferns can take the lack of light, and add a pop of green.

'I had a fixed idea of how I wanted the rooms to look,' Sean explains of his decor and indoor planting. 'I move things around, but always end up moving them back to where they were in the first place. Since I brought the taxidermy in here, it was, yes, this is the house for me.'

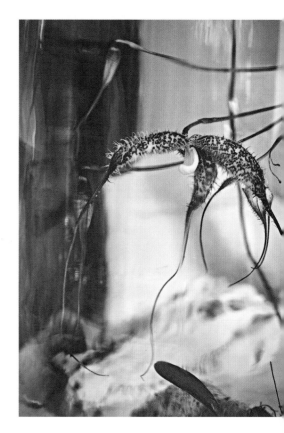

1 For added impact, group plants together. Not only do they look more effective, it also creates more humidity, which they love – especially in homes with central heating.

2 Don't worry about grouping like with like. Group plants by the conditions they thrive in, rather than by type.

3 To enjoy more delicate orchids from the greenhouse indoors for a few days, try placing them under domes with a bit of damp moss.

4 For an interesting and natural-looking way to display orchids, mosses and ferns, try mounting them on pieces of bark with a piece of string (the roots will eventually take hold), or inside a hollowed-out tree fern. These plants are epiphytes and would grow naturally on such surfaces, deriving their moisture from the air.

5 For a more attractive display indoors, hide a plastic pot with moss, hessian sacks or dead leaves.

6 For good results, position orchids in light, but avoid full sunshine. Cool temperatures and humidity work well. Orchids are exotic, so they can be hard to grow. This is part of the challenge!

7 Tap water is the enemy of orchids. Spray daily with rain-water instead.

'I DON'T THINK OF ORCHIDS AS PLANTS.
THEY'RE LIKE PETS. THERE ARE SO MANY THOUSANDS
OF THEM, IT'S ENDLESSLY FASCINATING.'

SEAN BARTON

THE EVERLASTING GRACE OF FLOWERS
Maggie Coker, Berlin, Germany

For centuries, flowers have been dried as a way of preserving them to create long-lasting flower arrangements that could be rearranged and combined in a fresh way. In this eclectic home belonging to a holistic mental wellness coach and floral stylist, preserved grasses and wildflowers make a rather chic comeback, taking centre stage to greet visitors with their striking shape and form. For this homeowner, the drive behind collecting and preserving flowers is more than perpetuating beauty. Having created a sanctuary that resonates with joyful emotion, her collection demonstrates reuse in action and a reverence for nature's gifts.

Maggie Coker has cultivated a bohemian vibe in her home, where dried flowers and grasses combine with vintage fabrics as a lead in the decoration. Having previously lived in Paris and London, she moved to Berlin, preferring the slower, greener pace of life.

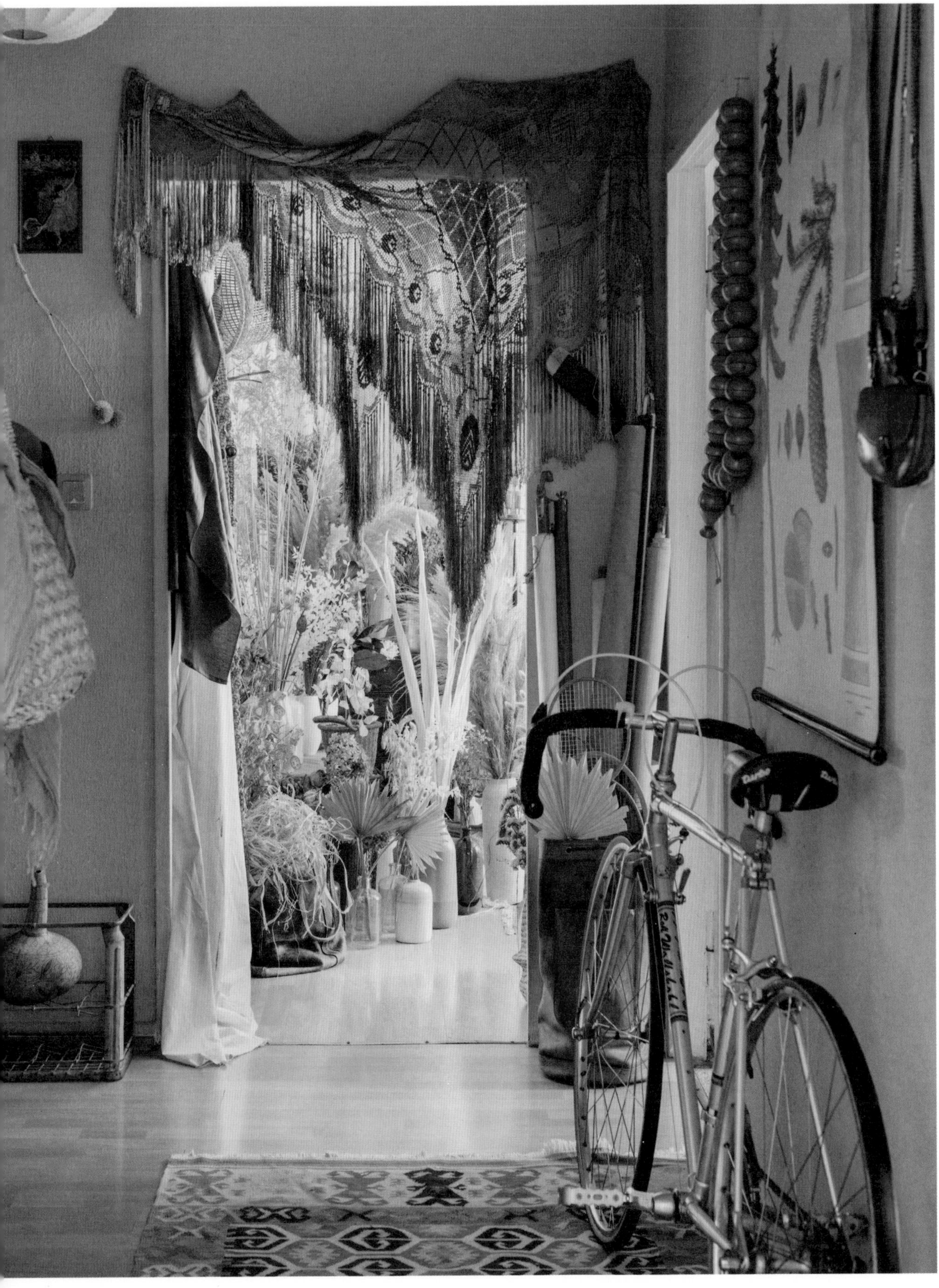

Calm, soothing, yet bursting with energy – Maggie's love of colour is visible everywhere in the house. In the hallway, straw hats hang on the wall, along with single-stem grasses. Palm grasses are propped up in the corner, chosen for their shape and height.

There's something beautiful about the colour and texture that occur when natural objects are dried. In this peachy-pink home in East Berlin, there are dried plants all around that started off green; when they died, they were kept for their strong shape and still look great. Maggie Coker, a botanical stylist and founder of FlowerTalk Berlin, uses the language of flowers as a tool to benefit mental wellness, as well as floral artistic expression. Flowers are part of her everyday life. 'They speak their own language,' she says. 'If you slow down and listen, you realize their magical therapeutic benefits.'

This creative, who notes that part of her collecting stems from the environment and not having the opportunity to replant, currently keeps palm leaves – 2 m (6½ ft) in height – in her living room, along with an array of vases containing pastel-dyed pampas grass, tall golden straw and *Lunaria annua* 'Honesty' laid out on the floor. Her do-not-ditch approach to floristry sees her drying poppies so delicate it is almost a miracle they stay together, along with fuller blooms such as roses and peonies, whose petals she gently prises apart to keep that fresh-flower feel.

'I like the texture of a dried flower,' she says of preserving these more moisture-loving plants. 'It's definitely about the form they take on, even the resilience. Technically, it's difficult. There are certain flowers that are born to be dried, but flowers whose stems hold a lot of water – these are tricky.'

There are several reasons why Maggie collects flowers and dries them. 'It's something that started years ago, while working as a florist,' she says, explaining how she would rescue flowers from the bins after a wedding or a big event. 'There is so much wastage in the flower industry. It's just a matter of time before people start questioning how much water use and land erosion goes into creating a lovely bouquet that usually ends up in the dustbin on day fourteen. And there are so many flowers that can't be used because they might have a wilted petal. For me, collecting is about respecting nature. I don't want to contribute to its waste.'

In a world that celebrates youthful freshness and shiny newness, she finds the process of preserving flowers a wonderful thing. 'For me, it is about making a statement that aging is beautiful – in people and plants – and we should appreciate these faded flowers,' she says. 'We are blessed to be in the presence of flowers. They are here in life to soothe us. They are nature's antidepressant.'

This idea connects with Maggie's childhood: 'When I was a kid, my mum was really sick, and as a result I was withdrawn and shy. I felt awkward in most situations outside of my home. From a young age, I realized that flowers had an effect on me. They could change my mood. I could get into a peaceful frame of mind and feel a lot happier. When I was about six, a neighbour gave me a rose from her garden. She was shocked as she had never seen me smile before – I couldn't believe its scent. To this day, I use rose fragrance in flower therapy. Whenever I've not been feeling so great, I put my trust in flower and plant therapy. It made a difference to my life, and took me out of moments of depression as a child. I've never looked back.'

But what makes a home? A house becomes a home when it blurs the lines between ourselves and our surroundings; it represents who we are and where we belong. Maggie describes her home as her sanctuary, reflecting her nomadic personality, her eclectic aesthetic, her profession and a collection of memories. Taking all these qualities, along with a stimulating colour palette in dusty peach and gold, it can lift the spirits even on a gloomy day. Add in the 'forever flower' factor, and the effect is one that is texturally layered with masses of character.

Dried flowers of all kinds appear throughout the house, yet Maggie's versatile creativity is most vividly expressed in the living room. On almost every wall, straw baskets have been combined with hops and grasses. Most of the furniture is secondhand and bought because she loved certain pieces – her justification for bringing them into the home.

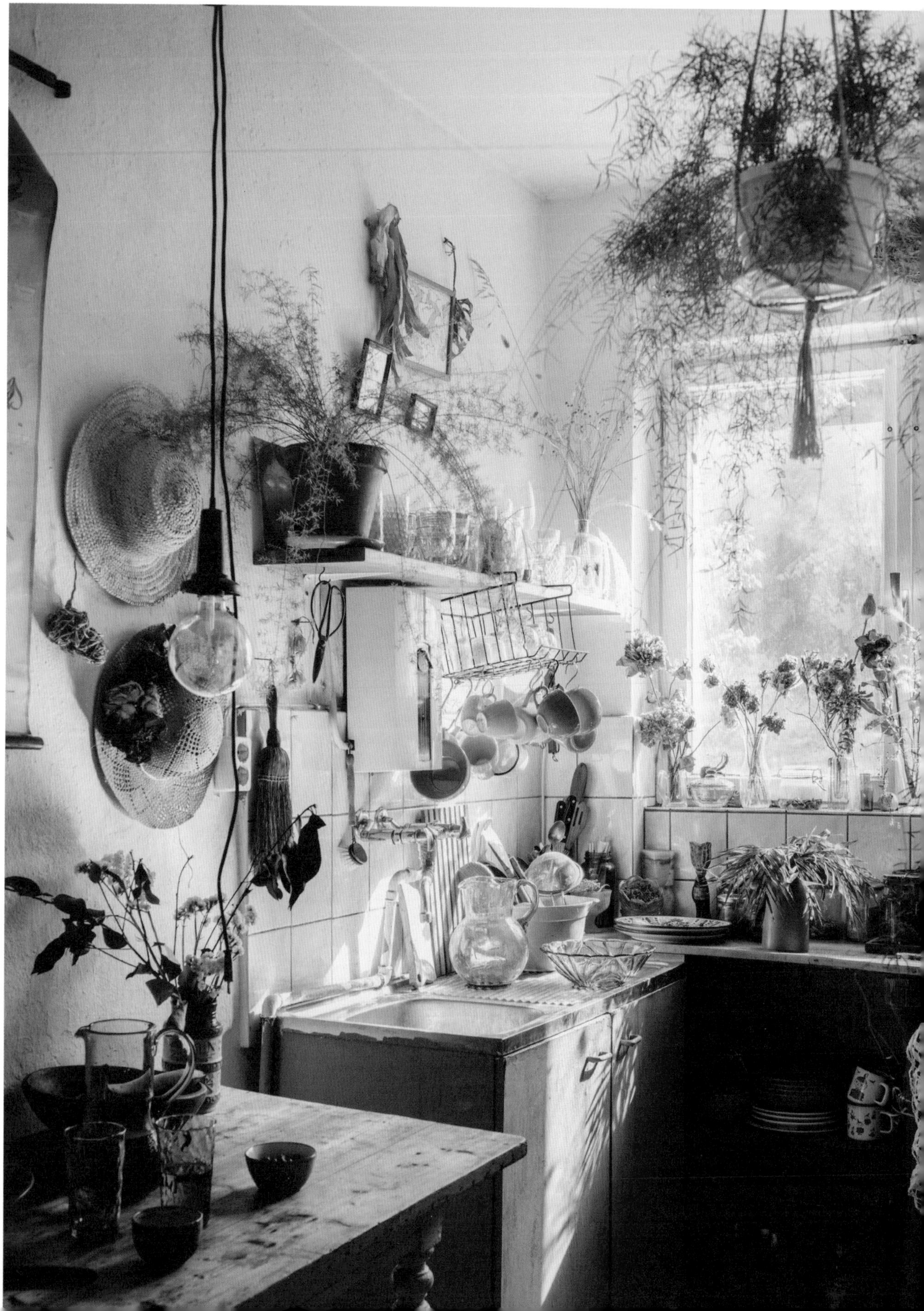

In the kitchen, there are flowers drying everywhere, whether strung along the wall or placed in vases. A combination of vintage amber and clear glass has been used, so that nothing blocks the light.

MAGGIE'S TIPS
FOR USING
DRIED FLOWERS
IN THE HOME

1 Find a dedicated spot to dry flowers. I use my kitchen. Sometimes I dry them upside down, sometimes I leave them as they are. I don't like to manipulate the flowers too much beyond expanding the petals to get a fuller shape, which shrinks as the flowers dry.

2 To keep roses from drying in too tight a shape, carefully open up the petals. Then it looks like a fresh flower again.

3 If you travel a lot, dried flowers are a great alternative to fresh ones. I like pampas grass, as it has a lot of personality, either dyed or faded. *Lunaria annua* 'Honesty' is one of my favourites, as it isn't easy to get or to dry.

4 To add colour to dried flowers, try using natural dyes. I use avocado to dye some of my grasses, boiling down the seeds to get the colour and then painting the condensed liquid onto leaves already bleached by the sun.

5 For better feng shui, I regularly dust the dried flowers, but also use a homemade cedarwood or eucalyptus spray to lift them and keep insects away.

6 For flowers that keep their colour, try delphiniums, peonies, hydrangeas and roses.

7 To make a natural potpourri, wild rose petals and lavender will keep their scent. I use essential oils to set the mood for the day and make cleansing sticks from dried sage and thyme, which I burn to change the energy of the space. My house smells great.

'FLOWERS SPEAK THEIR OWN LANGUAGE. IF
YOU SLOW DOWN AND LISTEN, YOU REALIZE THEIR
MAGICAL THERAPEUTIC BENEFITS.'

MAGGIE COKER

THE ART OF BONSAI
Raqib Shaw, London, UK

At this acclaimed artist's home and studio in south London, a forest of extraordinarily little trees are strategically housed under a purpose-built pergola. Twisted and turned to resemble plants in the wild, the miniature specimens are cultivated using the techniques of the Japanese art form of bonsai. Relishing in the comfort of routine while bowing to the majesty of nature, Raqib Shaw has learned to find balance in both. Here, he reflects on his bonsai guardianship and finding escapism in the world around him through art and the wonderment of dwarf trees. Beauty comes first.

There is a wonderful dichotomy in the care of bonsai. The individual specimens resemble windswept and ancient-looking trees, a look created by intensive manicuring to create a perfectly stunted form. 'There's nothing normal about bonsai,' Raqib says. 'Everything is controlled to the last detail, all to get an idea of something wild. I think it's fabulous.'

Scale is important when displaying a collection. At the entrance is a large indoor palm; in the Bonsai House, a prized miniature Chinese elm sits on a pedestal. Hanging planters of *Tradescantia zebrina* add to the sculptural mood, while in Raqib's yoga studio, a ficus with its twisted bark is strategically positioned next to a shrine for good humidity and light. Plants are aligned at right angles in a manner reminiscent of Mughal architecture.

The idea of using wood panelling to divide the space is Raqib's take on Japanese architecture. Made from European oak, these panels, along with the pretty pendant lights by Tom Raffield, cast shadows at night. 'When you look up in the evening, the shadows are like ballerinas dancing,' Raqib says. 'The Mughals used light and shadows in their gardens in the most fascinating way, an effect I was hoping to emulate here.'

When Raqib first acquired his beloved collection of bonsai – purchased from the estate of the great ornithologist, Dr Raymond Sawyer – he played classical music to bring the orphaned trees back to life. 'Not bang-bang music,' he says. 'Mozart is their favourite. I have a lovely violinist friend who would come over to play Mozart and Bach to them. I think that we as humans don't necessarily pay attention to the fact that plants and animals are capable of feeling things.'

As plants are sensitive and fragile, this need to nurture them is a strong part of their appeal. 'Bonsai are strange things,' Raqib notes of the discipline, mainly practised today by the elderly in Japan. 'You are supposed to pass them onto someone who will care for them the same way you did. It is very easy to kill a hundred years of hard work, and with that comes a great responsibility. I felt that because Dr Sawyer was not able to find the right person to look after his beloved bonsai, the universe chose me. I feel the urge to collect from a place of nurture. If I see a pristine bonsai, I don't say, oh, yes, I should have that. But if I see one that I feel needs a bit of help, care and undivided attention, that is the one I will choose. It's always the ones that are neglected that I like to look out for.'

Raqib's collection consists of a few dozen specimens. The Kimura juniper bonsai – the oldest tree he owns, from Masahiko Kimura, a bonsai master in Japan – is the star. 'I've never counted my bonsai,' he says. 'In Kashmir, they believe that if you have many children, you should not count them. You can't put a number on the fabulous things the so-called universe has given you.'

Raqib recalls how he was drawn to bonsai from a very young age. 'When I was about nine years old growing up in India, I attended an International Book Fair,' he explains. 'I remember there was a book with a bonsai on the cover, and I was fascinated by the fact that I thought it was a huge magnificent tree, only to realize that it was a bonsai.'

This interest developed over the years in conjunction with a study of Japanese culture, discipline and aesthetics, which goes hand-in-hand with Raqib's work as a practising artist. 'I have always been driven by aesthetics, and my interest in horticulture plays a significant part in this,' he says. 'Historically, Kashmir was embraced as heaven on earth by the Mughal emperors, and some of the greatest gardens of that period are there. That, coupled with my love of Capability Brown and the landscapes from 18th-century English literature, are my main inspirations.'

He continues: 'As a boy, I would look up at the maple trees. It's the same with the bonsai. If you look at them from below, you see a canopy. It is almost through the eyes of a child. They remind me of the nature of Kashmir, the mountain ranges and the trees that are hundreds and hundreds of years old. They remind me of home.'

Raqib describes his expansive studio as a 'garden of delights'. He rescued a former sausage factory in Peckham, south London, from ruin, and uses it as both a Renaissance-style atelier and his private living space. 'I wanted to go minimal, because everything else in my life is so excessive,' he says about the interior scheme. 'Kashmiris are uncomfortable with space, whereas the Japanese are the opposite. I was channelling the Japanese side of my aesthetics here.'

The large open spaces provide the perfect environment for creating art, as well as allowing Raqib to keep his extremely sensitive bonsai in the conditions they require. 'Living with them is important to me, as they need constant care,' he says of the temperamental and moody nature of his plants. 'You can't miss your watering spot. About four years ago, I went to Paris just for one day, but it was red-hot sunshine and one of my wonderful bonsai died.'

In the bonsai world, they say that until you kill your first bonsai, you can never be on the road to becoming a bonsai master. Nature's journey goes on.

'I WANTED TO GO MINIMAL, BECAUSE EVERYTHING ELSE IN MY LIFE IS SO EXCESSIVE.'

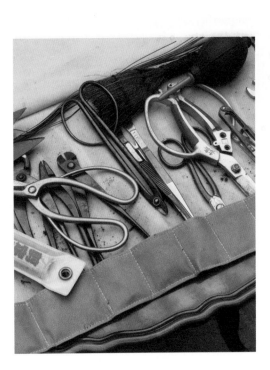

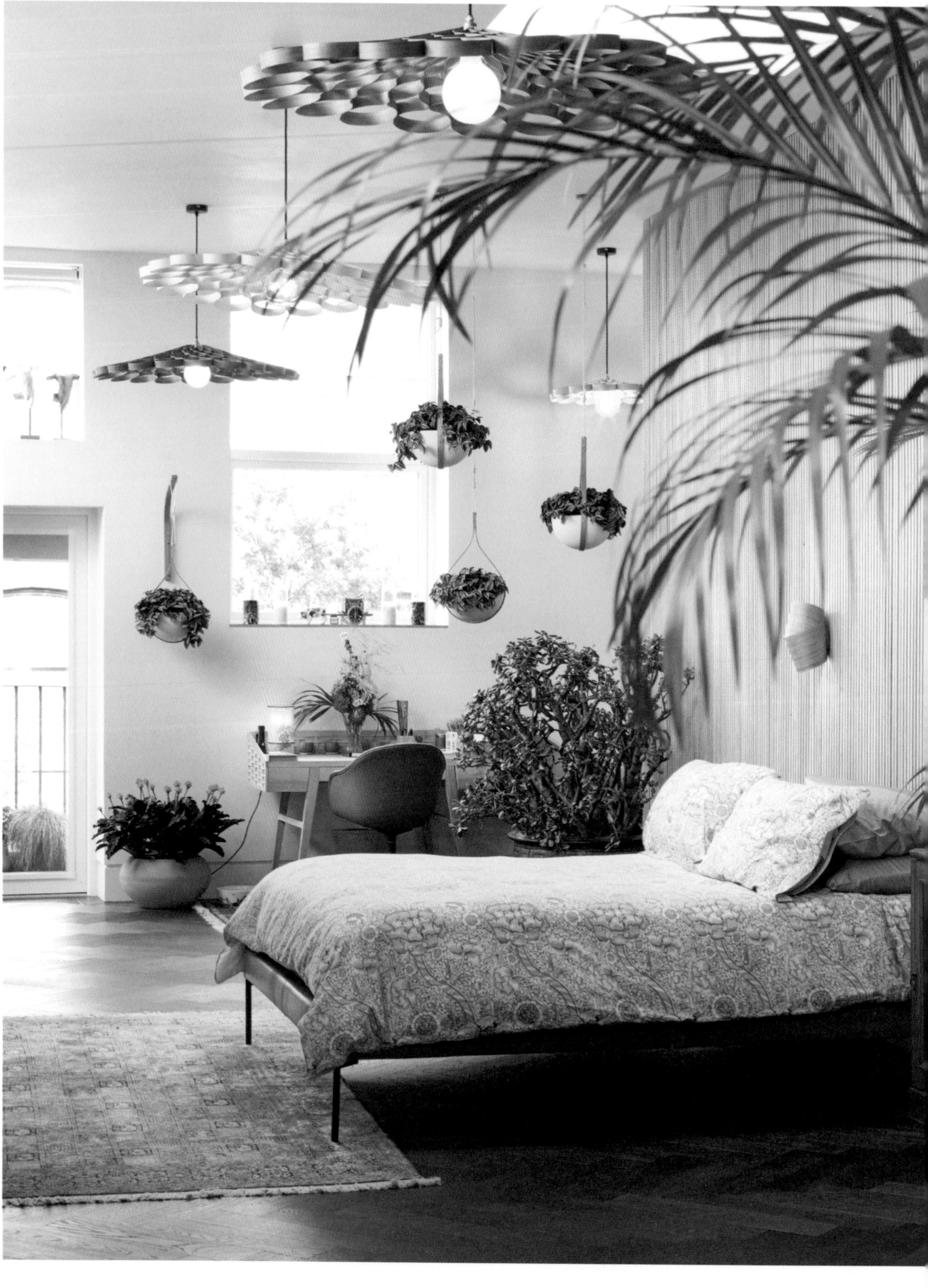

'LIVING WITH MY PLANTS IS IMPORTANT TO ME,
AS THEY NEED CONSTANT CARE.'

References to Kashmir and Persia appear throughout the house. The office space features an Ardabil carpet made from Kashmiri silk, which belonged to Raqib's grandfather. Favourite sculptural works are displayed in alcoves carved into the bathroom wall. 'Each object has its own energy, so it needs its own space,' Raqib says. 'Although I love clutter, it confuses the mind.'

1 Before buying a bonsai, consider whether you have the right place, time, dedication and patience to look after it. Are you willing to learn? Do you have a bonsai master living nearby? If you don't have these things, you're not going to do well. Don't buy a bonsai just because you like it. It is the same thing as if you were buying a dog.

2 To keep a bonsai well watered in winter, you don't have to worry about it for weeks. On a hot day in summer, however, you may need to water four times a day. The summer months are difficult.

3 Consistency is key. I water my bonsai religiously, but if someone else waters them, they actually become sad. You can see it.

4 For longevity, occasional root pruning is vital in encouraging new feeding roots.

5 To train a plant to the desired shape, try attaching copper wire to the trunk and branches, which can be gently pulled down and secured to the soil. Pruning is not a big deal for bonsai – it is the shaping that counts.

6 The first step in creating a bonsai is to move the plant to a container just large enough to hold the root ball. It will need to be repotted over time. It is extreme agony to the plant, but try to make it as gentle as possible. It is like open-heart surgery for me.

7 Remember that bonsai are not dwarf species. If you plant it in the ground, it is going to grow to the size of any other maple tree. It is like Chinese foot-binding.

'MY PLANTS REMIND ME OF THE NATURE OF KASHMIR, THE MOUNTAIN RANGES AND THE TREES THAT ARE HUNDREDS AND HUNDREDS OF YEARS OLD.'

DIRECTORY

PETER ADLER
pp. 106–15 *pebblelondon.com*

CHRISTINA AHLEFELDT-LAURVIG
pp. 168–77 *instagram.com/rensow.manor*

SEAN BARTON
pp. 188–97 *instagram.com/seansorchids*

KEVIN BEER
pp. 56–63 *instagram.com/hollywoodforeverkevin*

THOMAS BOOG
pp. 64–73 *thomasboog.com*

MAGGIE COKER
pp. 198–207 *mcvisualstyling.co.uk*

MICHELE OKA DONER
pp. 158–67 *micheleokadoner.com*

SPENCER FUNG
pp. 138–47 *spencerfung.co.uk*

OLIVER GUSTAV
pp. 116–25 *olivergustav.com*

EMMA HAWKINS
pp. 18–25 *instagram.com/emmahawkinsdsm*

BLOTT KERR-WILSON
pp. 74–83 *blottkerrwilson.com*

ZOE RUMEAU
pp. 36–43 *instagram.com/zoerumeau, instagram.com/atelierzoerumeau*

RAQIB SHAW
pp. 208–17 *raqibshawstudio.com*

SHHH MY DARLING
pp. 148–57 *shhhmydarling.com*

FERRY VAN TONGEREN
pp. 44–53 *finetaxidermy.com*

CAROL WOOLTON
pp. 96–105 *carolwoolton.com*

LUCA ZANAROLI
pp. 84–93 *lucazanaroli.com*

HUBERT ZANDBERG
pp. 26–35 *hzinteriors.com*

OTHER ARTISTS AND DESIGNERS

GRAEME BLACK
Fashion designer-turned-artist
graemeblack.com

DUNCAN CAMERON
2019 John Ruskin Prize finalist, artist and beekeeper
sharkcage.wixstie.com

LUCIE DE MOYENCOURT
South Africa-based artist of handmade ceramic shells
luciedemoyencourt.com

LYNDIE DOURTHE
French artist creating ethereal, delicate works in glass
lyndiedourthe.blogspot.com

PATRICK HAINES
British sculptor
patrickhainessculptor.com

LUCILLE LEWIN
London-based sculptor, working in porcelain and glass
lucillelewin.com

KATHERINE LLOYD
Shell and grotto artist
katherinelloyd.co.uk

DEAN PATMAN
Bristol-based sculptor using found materials
deanpatman.com

JANE PONSFORD
Artist and paper-maker
janeponsfordstudio.com

JOSEPH SCHEER
Photographer and printmaker
instagram.com/josephscheer

SHONA WILSON
Australian sculptor working with natural found materials
shonawilson.com

PLACES TO VISIT

FAIRBANKS MUSEUM AND PLANETARIUM

'A true gem of Victorian natural history tucked away in northern Vermont. It is an extraordinary place with displays of well over two dozen species of birds-of-paradise, along with many other specimens, exotic, extinct and indigenous.'
John Whitenight, collector and author

1302 Main Street, St Johnsbury, Vermont, USA *fairbanksmuseum.org*

LOUISIANA MUSEUM OF MODERN ART

'I discovered this museum a couple of years ago. It has a seamless relationship with nature and art through its architecture and surroundings. I didn't know galleries could be like this, and it is a place I often yearn to go back to.'
Lucy Augé, artist

Gl Strandvej 13, Humlebaek, Denmark *louisiana.dk*

LUIGI PIGORINI NATIONAL MUSEUM OF PREHISTORY AND ETHNOGRAPHY

'In Rome, five minutes from where I live, is an old-fashioned museum that hardly anyone knows about, with examples of ethnographic art from South America to the Pacific islands. I go every month to see all the artefacts I've come to know by heart since visiting as a child.'
Giano del Bufalo, antiques dealer

Palazzo Guglielmo Marconi 14, Rome, Italy *museocivilta.beniculturali.it*

MUSEE DE LA CHASSE ET DE LA NATURE

'When I first walked through the doors, I was convinced I had walked into a dream. Like entering a giant Wunderkammer, you are plunged into a world of art, poetry and exquisite taxidermy. It is a cerebral feast like no other.'
Simon Costin, curator, art director and designer

62 rue des Archives, Paris, France *chassenature.org*

MUSEO REGIONALE DI SCIENZE NATURALI

'Dario Lanzardo photographed this 17th-century museum for an exhibition in 1998, published in *Arca Naturae*. Rather than the usual celebrative capture of a museum and its contents, he was fascinated by how the animals and skeletons were stored. This is far more interesting for me.'
Napoleone Ferrari, curator, Museo Casa Mollino

Via Giolitti 36, Turin, Italy *mrsntorino.it*

MUSEUM NATIONAL D'HISTOIRE NATURELLE

'Located in the Jardin des Plantes, this museum has 68 million specimens in its collection, with 7,000 on display. The Grand Gallery of Evolution on the ground floor is pretty impressive and educational. They also have the most complete skeleton of a T-Rex and a mammoth.'
Hassan Abdullah, Les Trois Garçons

57 rue Cuvier, Paris, France *mnhn.fr/fr*

NATIONAL MUSEUM OF PRAGUE

'The museum's Hall of Minerals collection is one of my favourite places. It is over a hundred years old, with each mineral mounted in its original case and ebony black stand with its name in gold leaf on the base. I want them all!'
Tess Morley, shell artist

Václavské námesti 1700/68, Prague, Czechia *nm.cz*

PALEO GALLERIE

'After over thirty years travelling the world sourcing fossils and minerals, one of my favourite places to visit is this wonderful small museum in the south of France. Created by local wild man Luc Ebbo, his fossil collection is made special not just by the building it's housed in (an underground cellar in his house), but also by the meticulous presentation. Here, you can see extraordinary preservation of ichthyosaurs, crocodiles and mind-blowing spiny ammonite beds.'
Dale Rogers, founder, Dale Rogers Ammonite Gallery

Le Mardaric, Salignac, France *facebook.com/pg/Paleo-galerie*

THE SHELL MUSEUM

'This beautiful museum houses one of the finest shell collections in the UK. It is presided over by fiercely old-fashioned ladies who have no truck whatsoever with iPhones and photos – and they close for lunch. Aside from the glorious shells, it seems refreshingly undocumented and unbothered by Insta excess. I love it!'
Sue Skeen, artist, stylist and art director

Church House, Glandford, Norfolk, UK *shellmuseum.org.uk*

TEYLERS MUSEUM

'In 2018, when I was studying shell art in Amsterdam under the guidance of Niels van Alphen, I took a day off to visit the Teylers Museum in Haarlem. Established in 1778, it still resides in the beautiful original building. The well-preserved interior architecture with large display cabinets is half the experience. It is the perfect framework for the fossil room, the oval room, holding minerals and beautifully handcrafted scientific instruments.'
Mikael Hjärtsjö, shell artist, Shellman Scandinavia

Spaarne 16, Haarlem, Netherlands *teylersmuseum.nl*

WEALD & DOWNLAND LIVING MUSEUM

'If you're interested in architecture, nature and making things, this museum is maddeningly inspirational. Rolling hills and talent abound.'
Harriet Anstruther, interior designer

Town Lane, Singleton, West Sussex, UK *wealddown.co.uk*

A LA RONDE

This quirky, sixteen-sided house in Devon is fabulous in many ways, but in particular for its shell gallery and staircase, created by the sister-owners Jane and Mary Parminter in the 1800s.

Summer Lane, Exmouth, Devon, UK *nationaltrust.org.uk*

MARIANNE NORTH GALLERY

This vivid collection of 19th-century botanical art in Kew Gardens is a total treat for anyone interested in plant illustration. The display of 800 paintings cover the walls and show the plants in context of their landscape and is full of colour.

193 Kew Road, Richmond, UK *kew.org*

SIR JOHN SOANE'S MUSEUM

The home of Regency architect Sir John Soane is a shrine to his vast collections of paintings, sculpture, architectural fragments and furniture. It is an inspiration on the power of objects and how they can spark creativity.

13 Lincoln's Inn Fields, London, UK *soane.org*

VIKTOR WYND MUSEUM OF CURIOSITIES

In a smaller-scale vein to the Horniman Museum in Forest Hill, south London, this Hackney basement world of wonder displays marvels of the natural and scientific world, from dodo bones to rare and unusual taxidermy.

11 Mare Street, London, UK *thelasttuesdaysociety.org*

PLACES TO SHOP

DAVID AYRE

'This is one of my favourite shops. David has an interesting collection focusing on diorama of birds from the different continents and he tends to sell rare specimens.'
Hassan Abdullah, Les Trois Garçons
27 Old Gloucester Street, London, UK *ayreandco.com*

PETERSHAM NURSERIES

'Dinner is delightful, the café is great and there's some very inviting retail therapy too – all in a really lovely setting.'
Lucinda Chambers, co-founder, Collagerie
Church Lane, off Petersham Road, Richmond, UK *petershamnurseries.com*

TAGE ANDERSEN

'This magical floral shop and gallery in central Copenhagen has been a huge influence on me since discovering it, aged sixteen. As you walk down the stairs and take in the scents and colours, it is like stepping into a fairytale.'
Steiner Berg-Olsen, antiques dealer and floral designer
Ny Adelgade 12, Copenhagen, Denmark *tage-andersen.com*

THE ARKENSTONE

Dallas-based collector Dr Robert Lavinsky's online mineral store and event listing.
irocks.com

DEYROLLE

Most known for its collection of taxidermy, this is a Paris institution for nature enthusiasts.
deyrolle.com

EVOLUTION

A landmark in New York's SoHo district, specializing in science and natural history-related collectibles.
theevolutionstore.com

LIBRAIRIE ALAIN BRIEUX

This lovely old bookstore on the Left Bank is a gem for old science and natural-history books and prints.
alainbrieux.com

LINDA FENWICK

An online go-to for shellwork accessories, from jewelled clam shells to coral bookends.
lindafenwickshellsindesign.com

THE MERCHANT'S TABLE

Handcrafted objects by independent British makers and artists, including items such as bronze mushrooms, botanical casts, scallop-shell brass tea lights and willow baskets.
themerchantstable.co.uk

SAINT VERDE BOTANICALS

Founder Neville Trickett is a natural-born collector, a passion that extends to the legacy of this nursery in Durban, South Africa.
svbotanicals.co.za

SHE'S LOST CONTROL

London mineral seller with a Sustainable Mining Initiative.
sheslostcontrol.co.uk

THE SOCIETY INC

Founded by Sydney-based stylist Sibella Court, and known for its amazing collection of nature-inspired hardware such as scallop-shaped door knockers and beachcombing curiosities.
thesocietyinc.com.au

VENUSROX

A showroom in the Notting Hill neighbourhood of London, devoted to fine crystals and crystal jewelry.
venusrox.com

PLACES FOR INSPIRATION

BEACHES OF MADAGASCAR

'The beaches on the west coast are among the most beautiful natural environments I have ever seen. I have never seen a plastic bottle or trace of tar, but I have seen whales and dolphins swimming undisturbed in those wonderful waters. The residents still move around in canoes, using paddles or sails, and rarely a motor. Tourism is concentrated in just a few islands. I truly hope this paradise remains as immaculate as it is now.'

Barnaba Fornasetti, artistic director, Fornasetti Atelier

HARROGATE FLOWER SHOW

'Harrogate is a Georgian spa town, and my hometown. It also has a flower show each year. After strolling past the storybook giant gunnera, a heart-lifting display of dahlias can be found, some of which are so large they look you straight in the eye from heads as big as your own.'

Georgie Hopton, artist

Great Yorkshire Showground, Harrogate, North Yorkshire, UK

LOGAN ROCK BEACH

'I love walking on the beach here, near Land's End. It's the most beautiful place, with steep granite cliffs, the sea rolling in below and seagulls flying above. It has a pinkish sand – basically crushed seashells – with many types of seaweed and driftwood, lichen and moss. The natural world is best seen outside of galleries and museums, in my view.'

James Hepworth

Logan Rock, Treen, Cornwall, UK

SCOTT'S GROTTO

'This fascinating series of tunnels and underground chambers, built in the 18th century and decorated with shells, flint and glass, was one of the first grottoes I visited when I was starting out on my career. I took a day trip from London and wandered around the grotto with a rare, almost spiritual feeling that I was on the right path in life.'

Katherine Lloyd, shell artist

28/34 Scott's Road, Ware, Hertfordshire, UK

UBUD, BALI

'There are places that call to us. For me, that place is Bali. It has gained a pretty rotten reputation from being over-hyped and crowded, but it remains sacred ground that I head to whenever I have the time or opportunity. My favourite places are the spectacular water temples you find all over the island, or a series of caves and waterfalls, a holy spot outside Ubud. I've had incredible spiritual experiences, where I can feel and remember what it means to be truly free.'

JJ Martin, founder, La Double J

OTHER RESOURCES

EVENTS AND COURSES

Bart's Pathology Museum
qmul.ac.uk
British Academy of Taxidermy
thebritishacademyoftaxidermy.org
Kettle's Yard, University of Cambridge
kettlesyard.co.uk
Orchid Society of Great Britain
osgb.org.uk
Tucson Gem and Mineral Show
tgms.org/show

WHAT TO READ

Hazelle Jackson, *Shell Houses and Grottoes*
Shire Publications, Oxford, 2001
Martina Mondadori Sartogo, *Cabana: Anthology*
Vendome Press, London, 2018
Carol Woolton, *The New Stone Age: Ideas and Inspiration for Living with Crystals*
Ten Speed Press, Berkeley, California, 2020
Umberto Pasti and Ngoc Minh Ngo, *Eden Revisited: A Garden in Northern Morocco*
Rizzoli, New York, 2019
Madeleine Pinault, *The Painter as Naturalist: From Dürer to Redoute*
Flammarion, Paris, 1991
Hugh Stix, Marguerite Stix and R. Tucker Abbott, *The Shell: Five Hundred Million Years of Inspired Design*
Harry N. Abrams, New York, 1969
Jaap Sinke and Ferry van Tongeren, *Darwin, Sinke and van Tongeren: Our First Book*
Lannoo Publishers, Tielt, 2018
The Mineralogical Record
mineralogicalrecord.com
John Whitenight, *Under Glass: A Victorian Obsession*
Schiffer Ltd, Atglen, Pennsylvania, 2013

INDEX

Page numbers in *italics* refer to illustrations

Many thanks to the team at Thames & Hudson, especially Fleur Jones, for believing in the idea and nurturing its progress into realization. Thank you, of course, to everyone featured – and plenty of others besides – who generously gave their time and knowledge while writing the book, of which I am hugely proud. I am so grateful to all contributors who allowed me to rifle through personal collections, but also the many others who helped steer me along the way with ideas and inspiration. The experience was full of positivity and collaboration. Special thanks to Sean Barton for the loan of his precious books. Thank you to Blott Kerr-Wilson for her hospitality as well as letting me loose in her shell-laden home. I'm indebted to photographers from all over the world for their help in bringing this book to life. Their imagery captures the beauty of the collections and I am lucky to feature their work alongside mine. Biggest thanks as always to my family and friends for their endless support and encouragement wherever my story enthusiasms go. For Josephine, let's always gather shells and pebbles from the beach.

Claire Bingham is an interiors journalist and author who has been finding, writing about and photographing amazing homes for almost twenty years. Previously the homes editor of *Elle Decoration*, she writes about interiors, travel, perfume and food for publications worldwide including *Vogue Italia*, *Sunday Times Style*, *Architectural Digest* and *Grazia*. She is the author of many books; her first with Thames & Hudson, *Wild Kitchen*, was published in 2020.

PHOTO CREDITS
2, 6–7, 96–104, 106–14, 208–16 Chris Tubbs; 9, 74–82, 188–96 Claire Bingham; 13, 116–24 Mike Karlsson Lundgren; 14–15, 158–66 Ngoc Minh Ngo; 18–24 Simon Upton; 26–34 Simon Upton/Interior Archive; 36–42, 64–72 Virginie Garnier; 44–52 Carlfried Verwaayen; 56–62, 126–35 Tim Hirschmann; 84–92 Christian Schaulin; 138–46 Martin Morrell; 148–56 Marta Puglia; 168–76 Krautkopf; 180–7 Annie Schlecter; 198–206 Robert Rieger; 215 (bottom) Raqib Shaw, *Self Portrait in the Study at Peckham (after Vincenzo Catena)*, 2015–16, courtesy of the artist and White Cube

For mum (the classifier), for dad (the hoarder)

On the cover: The entrance hall in Ferry van Tongeren's home in Haarlem, Netherlands (photo: Carlfried Verwaayen)

First published in the United Kingdom in 2022 by Thames & Hudson Ltd, 181A High Holborn, London WC1V 7QX

First published in the United States of America in 2022 by Thames & Hudson Inc., 500 Fifth Avenue, New York, New York 10110

Designed by Apartamento Studios

British Library Cataloguing-in-Publication Data
A catalogue record for this book is available from the British Library

Library of Congress Control Number 2021943317

ISBN 978-0-500-024003

Printed in China by Shenzhen Reliance Printing Co. Ltd

FSC
MIX
Paper from responsible sources
www.fsc.org FSC® 0000000

Be the first to know about our new releases, exclusive content and author events by visiting
thamesandhudson.com
thamesandhudsonusa.com
thamesandhudson.com/au